BISON
BOOKS

Delphine Red Shirt

Bead on an Anthill

A Lakota Childhood

University of Nebraska Press
Lincoln and London

© 1998 by the
University of Nebraska Press
All rights reserved
Manufactured in the United
States of America

⊗

First Bison Books printing: 1999

Library of Congress Cataloging-
in-Publication Data
Red Shirt, Delphine, 1957–
Bead on an anthill:
a Lakota childhood /
Delphine Red Shirt.
p. cm.
ISBN 0-8032-3908-4
(cloth: alk. paper)
ISBN 0-8032-8976-6
(paper: alk. paper)
1. Red Shirt, Delphine, 1957–
—Childhood and youth.
2. Teton Indians—Biography.
I. Title.
E99.T34R337   1998
973'.049752'0092—dc21
[B]
97-14418   CIP

This book is dedicated to Richard,
to our wakᶜ ąyeża
Justin, Megan, and Kirsten,
and to Wįyą Isnala, Ina mitᶜ awa kį he e,
nahą, Pte Oyate, hena kį iyu ha.

A man from the north gave me a cane
I told this girl so.

She will live to be old
Her tribe will live.

[A song from the "Tʻatʻąka olową pi," a ceremony
performed for a young girl when she reaches womanhood.]

Contents

Acknowledgments

I am grateful to Richard Harding Shaw, my husband of twenty years, for his astute observations, his comments, and his undaunted belief in me.

I am deeply indebted to Howard R. Lamar, Sterling Professor of History and former president of Yale University, for his interest and support.

I am grateful for the material collected by James R. Walker and made available through the Colorado Historical Society. I am grateful for the Lakota voice of George [Long Knife] Sword, which is present in the material collected by Walker. I am grateful for the documents retained by the Colorado Historical Society that are written in the Lakota language, the language of my true self.

I am grateful for the *Lakota-English Dictionary: A Dictionary-oie wowapi wan of Teton Sioux*, which was compiled by Eugene Buechel sj.

I wish to thank Charlotte G. Currier, for being first a teacher and second, a critic. In addition, I would like to thank Barbara MacEachern, Wesleyan University, for her guidance in the beginning.

I would like to thank the following people for reading the manuscript and offering constructive comments: Joe Starita, Allen Trachtenberg, and Richard Kislik.

Introduction

I wrote these stories primarily for the joy of remembering what was good in my life. I wanted to remember these things, to write them down, the old Lakota words and my connection to the world around me through them. These stories are told through the eyes of my childhood but from an adult perspective. They are what I remember; "Weksuye" meaning "I remember"; "Ciksuye" meaning "I remember you"; "Miksuye" meaning "remember me."

In the process of writing these stories, I felt great satisfaction in reconnecting to my native language, Lakota. I felt at home using it and I felt gratified speaking it again. It came alive for me and brought back all the feelings I felt as a child when I first heard those words spoken. When I began to write using Lakota, I was not sure how its use would come across to the reader. How effective it would be to use my native language to capture the essence of what my culture means to me and of what I wanted to convey about it to the reader. I know now that my writing was richer for its use.

It is a custom in my tribe to begin any public speech or presentation with an autobiographical statement, giving my status in the tribe and telling why I am qualified to speak. In keeping with this tradition, I will only say that there was nothing special about my life except for the fact that I was a Lakota wakˈąyeża, a child, born to a strong Lakota mother and gentle father, the two people who gave me my identity. I am grateful to them and to my Lakota ancestors for the right to say in Lakota, "Le mįye," meaning "this is who I am."

Beads on an Anthill

I remember how I once followed an ant home. When I was a child, I was able to do things that seem preposterous to me now. But as a small child, I stayed close to the ground and imagined all sorts of possibilities. I followed the ant home because I needed glass beads to make a ring, a simple string of beads to decorate my finger after the metal washer I had put on it had caused the finger to swell. My father had to take me to the appliance store on Main Street. The appliance service man, who also sold stoves, refrigerators, and washers, used a small clipper to snip it off my swollen finger, the finger I had wanted to adorn with something pretty and shiny. I was determined to find or make a ring, one that would not make my finger swell. So I decided to make one out of brightly colored beads.

It was common knowledge among the children in my neighborhood, and some of the adults as well, that the ants collected our discarded beads and carried them home. So, I followed an ant home. In Nebraska the roads are hard-packed, and the dirt is an off-white color. I followed the ant up the hill past my great-aunt's house and to the trail behind her house where the road ended and tall weeds grew in clumps. It was easy for the ant to make its way through what must have seemed to it a forest of tall trees. I followed it past clumps of dirt, a few discarded potato chip bags, and broken glass to the ant pile it called its home. There the other ants milled about on a mound that rose about four or five inches from the ground. The mound had one hole in the center, and around this opening, scattered about like planned landscaping, were small round rocks and beads. Beads of all colors. I remember the blue, pale green, yellow, red, and even the white beads that were scattered about the opening, childlike decorations or offerings to a god. I watched the ant enter the pile, and then I lost track of it. It had led me to what I wanted, and I forgot it immediately.

I patiently watched the ants entering and exiting the mound in a rhythmic way. I could have sat on my haunches or heels on that hot summer's day and watched the ants forever. Instead I carefully picked out the beads I wanted for my ring. I worked carefully and slowly, watching the ants run from the pincers my small fingers formed, in order to fish out the best beads. I didn't want to disturb them. I was as afraid of them as they were of me. I was afraid particularly of the red ants, afraid of their pincers and the way they attach themselves to you securely before stinging you.

I selected the best beads, the unbroken ones. I often wonder how they carried those beads up the hill from our neighborhood to their mound. Did they take turns carrying them, or did they just pick them up securely and walk for days to reach their pile? How persistent they were in stealing the beads from us, as persistent as we were in stealing them back. That day I raided the anthill, I took all their blue and yellow beads. I walked away without a twinge of guilt, the beads in my hand, ready to find a needle and thread. I don't remember being cruel by messing up their pile with my foot or a stick. I only remember taking what I wanted and waiting for another day to find the colors I wanted that they didn't have that day.

I carefully carried the beads home in my small hand. I saw my aunt sitting underneath a tall cottonwood tree. She held a small bowl in her lap. An inch or so of multicolored beads covered the bottom of the bowl. She did what others in our neighborhood did: she "waksu," or "beaded." The Lakota word for bead is "psit'o." The word for beading is "ksu," which sounds like "K-show." My aunt beaded well. She worked on a loom, a small wooden frame about a foot long, with a width of six inches. It resembled a stringed instrument, something like a violin only strung with nylon thread. The player is the beader who picks out the beads on her needle in a combination that will add to the design that is already on the loom, or she may begin a new pattern. She moves across the strings as if to play the violin strings with a bow, places the beads between the threads, and returns back through to secure them. The wooden frame my aunt worked on so patiently held a white beaded band with bold geometric designs on it. She created her own design the way a composer writes music or an artist paints a picture. She worked methodically and looked carefully to fish out the right combination of beads from the bowl, the same way I fished out the beads from the anthill. I preferred the beads that were the color blue, "t'o," we say in Lakota.

It wasn't until I was older that I learned that all beads are carefully mixed before beading. The different colors are not kept separately because it was thought that each bead had its own power; if combined, no one bead would have power over any other bead. Today when I bead, I am tempted to keep the colors separate in order to make it easier. If I kept all the blue, yellow, white, and red beads, each color in its own separate container, it would be easier to find the different colors when I need them. I sometimes give in to the temptation, but then I remember my aunt patiently fishing out her colors, and I, with a strange abandon, throw all the separate colored beads together into one bowl. In the same way the ants were compelled to carry the useless beads home, I find myself compelled to follow in the footsteps of my ancestors.

Years later, I heard a story from my aunt about her and my uncle. When they were first married, they took long walks in the hills around the place where my uncle grew up, near where I lived on the reservation. She said that once when she and my uncle walked behind the first set of hills and continued onto a second set beyond the set you can see from the road, they found an old burial ground. She said a family must have been buried there, buried in traditional dress: in buckskin dresses, shirts, leggings, moccasins, and perhaps necklaces, armbands, and other items decorated in the finest quillwork or beadwork. She said that children, or little girls, were often buried with their dolls dressed in beadwork, or with other toys. She told me that near the burial ground stood the largest anthill she had ever seen. On that anthill she remembers seeing the beads of many colors piled high, old beads that the ants had collected.

I remember climbing those hills, up past the "peẑiħota," or "sage," and the tall grass. Up high, where the pine trees grow along the ridge. I remember how the pine trees seemed to sing in the high wind. It was said long ago that the spirit world lies far beyond the pine trees. When the people talked about the spirit world, they would always point north, and they would say "waẑiyata," which means "north" beyond the pines. What I remember most about the pine trees in the hills near where I grew up is the strong scent of pine in the summer heat. As a child I would sit in the shade of those pine trees and carefully take apart the pine needles, then make them into necklaces and other jewelry. Today, I've lost the patience for doing such things, lost the patience for making the finest jewelry with whatever is on hand.

In my adolescence, someone gave me a black paper box filled with brown-gray porcupine hair and quills. On certain days I would bring out the box of quills and stare at them, knowing I needed to do something with them, but I didn't know what. The quills called to me, pulling at me, and I kept answering in a helpless way. I kept examining them. I didn't know what to do with them. Had I lived a hundred years earlier, I would have known what to do: my mother would have shown me. I would have sorted the quills by size, knowing that the largest and coarsest quills come from the back and tail of the porcupine; these I would save and use for larger pieces I wanted to decorate, such as a cradleboard for my daughter. The slender and delicate quills come from the neck of the porcupine and the finest quills from the belly of the animal. I would use the finest quills to decorate an armband or a pair of moccasins. I would store them in a buffalo bladder and care for them as an artist would care for her paints and brushes. When I was ready to use them, I would have taken the quills and worked them carefully through my teeth, thereby flattening them, and dyed them in order to use them the way I use beads today. I would boil them with buffalo berries and dock root until I saw the bright red I needed. I would boil them with sunflower and pieces of dry oak bark or roots of the cattail, to get yellow. I would boil the quills with wild grapes to get the color black, the colors red, yellow, and black being the only ones we used before beads were available. These colors are our sacred colors—red, yellow, black, and white. I would have used sinew for string and would have made decorations with the red, yellow, and black quills as easily as I now create patterns with beads, patterns that resemble the finest embroidery. I would not have been able to use blue quills. Not until the traders brought blankets and bolts of cloth were we able to dye the quills blue. It was said we boiled the quills with bits of blue blanket to get the color we wanted. I prefer the color blue to any other color.

The quills of porcupines are thin and sharp. If a curious dog had the misfortune of getting too close to a porcupine, it soon found itself in pain when the quills of the small animal lodged themselves in the dog's face. I have seen such dogs and do not envy those who have to remove the quills. The quills I had in my possession were from a porcupine that had tried to cross the highway and had not survived. The quills I had were ivory-colored with black tips. How patient I would have had to be, had I lived a hundred years ago, to have taken them as they were and worked them through my teeth to soften them. I am not so patient today. It was said that we women were the only ones who knew how to do quillwork. We decorated our lives with quillwork. A quillwork cradleboard, a hundred or so years ago, would have been worth one horse. We women, in our way, vied with men for their most prized possession, a horse.

A hundred years later, I know how to bead, how to combine all the colors and string the beads on the loom. I know how to pay tribute when I bead, to that mystery which underlies all things, by inserting the odd bead of a different color into my otherwise perfect creation. The one bead of imperfection signifies my own imperfection, acknowledges that only the Creator is perfect, that only His creations bear the mark of perfection. In my Lakotaness, I imitate my Creator with humility, my ego set aside as always. I even know which designs belong to my people and which are from the "t'oka," or "other peoples." The one thing I do not know is how to practice the art that would have bound me to my grandmother, my great-grandmother, and to my great-grandmother's grandmother. I do not know how to work the quill through my teeth to soften it. I do not know how to dye it until it absorbs the color of chokecherry juice and then to string it with sinew and with great patience sew it onto my daughter's cradleboard. Someday I will teach myself, and when I do, I will teach my daughter and she will teach her daughter and in that way I will reconnect the circle that binds me to them and to my mother's mother.

I was taught as a child that even the ant has its place in creation. That was why I was told to tell a spider, "K'ola, wakįyą agli," meaning "Friend, thunder has come," before I killed it, should I be forced to kill it. The spider's bite could make me sick, and I must always respect it. The Lakota words "mak'a aką mani" when translated mean "earth-upon-it-dwells and walks," and all things, including the ant, that dwell upon the earth are sacred because all things have a spirit. The living spirit of all living things is called "oni," and the spirit of the dead is called "wanaġi." I did not understand the word "oni" as a child, but I knew the word "wanaġi," which meant "ghost" to me and all children, and I dreaded the thought of seeing one.

All things have a spirit, it is said, because everything is a part of that which is "Taku Śką Śką"—meaning "that which moves, that which lives and is connected." "Taku Śką Śką" is the mystery within all living things, which is sacred energy and is "wak'ą" or "divine." It connects us, the ant and me. We are all on the same spiritual plane, equal and justly so. No one is greater than any other. One is closer to the ground than the other, but even then, one still has to bow to the other. "Tʻažuśka kį he woųspe ni cu oki hi," it is said, meaning "it is possible that an ant can teach you a valuable lesson."

The closest words to "love" in our Lakota language are "ųśla," meaning "compassion or pity," and "tʻehila," meaning to "value or be unwilling to part with." Where love is concerned, the heart is always referred to in our language and the word "good," or "waśte." I remember the words "Mi cąte el cį yu ha" or "in my heart I have put you," in referring to love. I remember the words because it is in "my cąte," "my heart," that I have put all those things that I like to remember best, like my aunt beading underneath a tall cottonwood shimmering in the summer sun, outside of my mother's house in Nebraska. She took pity on me. She must have thought "śika ųśilaye" when she saw me. The way my mother implored me to do, "wa ųśilaye," "-ye" in the feminine voice, to me, her daughter. She would implore me to have compassion, to have pity on the smallest ant, the smallest child, the oldest person, the feeblest person, even the person considered the strongest, to pity her, to pity myself, "wa ųśilaye." In the same way my aunt stringing her beads took pity on me that day. "Hiyu we," she said, "come over here," when she saw me with the dusty pile of beads in my hand. She pried my hand open and took the beads, chuckling as she did so. In a matter of minutes she had transformed my pile into a slender string of alternating colors of yellow and blue beads. She measured my finger, counted the exact number of beads, cut and tied the string off, making a perfect ring for a small finger.

Years later, I turned over a rock in the thick woods of a forest and saw not red ants, but large black ants. I felt great pity for them. They ran frantically, trying to carry small white eggs to shelter. They ran in great confusion, each carrying an egg, putting eggs here and there. I felt sorry for them, but I had lost that feeling I had for them when I was little and raided their anthill for the treasure they had accumulated. I had lost that feeling of admiration and fear I had when I visited them and took what I needed from them. I was no longer afraid, only sorry that I somehow, if wrongly, perceived their insignificance in the world I was standing in.

Le Ina mitąwa ką e,
That Mother of Mine

I grew up with aunts, uncles, cousins, and various relatives and
neighbors who have permeated all that I have become. These in-
dividuals, whose lives seemed to me as a young girl to appear in a
flash and then disappear, made a deep and lasting impression upon
my life. They, in that moment they appeared, became a part of my
consciousness forever.

I remember standing next to my mother as she sat comfortably
in a chair with her hands in her wide, deep lap, listening to a relative or neighbor telling her something. My mother listens well.
She can give the impression of one holding court. A massive
woman with strong legs and arms, she sits in her throne of flesh.
There is nothing small or demure about my mother. As a small
child she appeared to me to be large, strong, and capable.

I developed, from my first conscious moment, in a world
forged by this strong and able woman that I call "Mom-mah." In
her lifetime, Mom-mah had eleven children, three of whom died
in infancy. Out of her eight living children, including five daughters and three sons, I did not stand out in any particular way. Although we shared the same mother, we were not aware as children
that some of us had a different father. At one point or another, we
all lived under the same roof as children, and everyone remembered my mother in a separate and distinct way. We each had our
own memories with which to deal. For a long time I did not look

back. I did not want to look back at my life from the present moment and find blame.

I look at my mother today as she was back then, even though
she is now smaller and her arms and legs thinner and considerably
weaker. I see her as she was in that moment when I first became
conscious of her as a child—at her kitchen table, talking to a relative or neighbor, with me standing by her side. "Okʿo śkata ye,"
"go play," she told me, nudging me toward the door. Play? I must
have hesitated because she said again in a sterner voice, "Śkata ye
ni wakʿąyeża kśto," meaning "Why don't you go play. You are a
child." The fact that she used the word "kśto" indicated to me
that she was asserting something which she knew I was doubting.
It startled me, because even as a child I thought I was to be considered in the light of my consciousness. I had that acute feeling
of observing the world without judgment and shame, and only a
need to know what it is I am here for and what it is I need to know.
Even then, I felt keenly aware and painfully inquisitive, afraid I
would miss something if I wasn't present in the moment. I ob-
served the world then without judgment or shame, only an intense
need to know what it was that I was here for and what it was that
I needed to know.

I must have considered myself, at the age of five or six, to be an
extension of my mother. Whenever I was near her, listening and
observing, I felt whole. Whenever I became conscious of myself
alone with a sibling or playmate, I do not remember that same
feeling or the need for human contact that I felt with Mom-mah.
I did not fear her, and I did not feel safe around some of the older
kids in the neighborhood. In my mother I had a haven, a space
where I could be near her and feel reassuringly safe. She often did
not have time for an individual child. She preferred the company
of adults, but I preferred her presence more than anyone else's. It
must have been that feeling of being safe which I equate with this
woman.

I know now that many of my siblings, particularly my sisters,
did not share the same feelings I had growing up with Mom-mah.

I often wonder if my mother was like the sun, and we were like the earth, each of us in her large family receiving the powerful rays of the sun at our specific positions relative to her, she being our sun and universe. If that were the case, what latitude did I occupy? A position on the earth where the sun's rays are only neutral, neither too harmful nor highly beneficial. When I think of the impact she had on my early life and of my consciousness of her aura of safety, I wonder how it is that I have turned out to be who I am.

I used to believe in myself as a young child. Every night I went to sleep thinking that tomorrow I would be bigger and better than I had been the day before. I always fell asleep facing the wall near Mom-mah, who slept on the side away from the wall where she could rise easily in the morning without waking my younger brother and me. My brother slept between me and Mom-mah. We slept with her after my younger sister died, after my father walked away one day and didn't return for many years. There was more room in Mom-mah's bed for my brother and me.

I ran after my father the day he walked away. I ran a quarter of a mile up the dirt road leading to the highway. "Dad-dee," I called. "Dad-dee, tokiya la he?" I asked him. "Where are you going?" He stopped and looked back at me, his hands in his pockets, and said, "Daughter, I'm going away." He always said "daughter" to me in English. He, unlike my mother, preferred English and rarely spoke to us in Lakota. He continued walking with his long strides, his hat perched upon his head just so, and his French blood showing in his thin face and long thin nose. He looked back at me as I struggled to keep up with him. I asked him, "Taku we?" I wanted to know "why?" because I somehow felt that it was my fault that he was going away. He shrugged and continued walking. "Your mother is a hard woman to get along with," he said. I walked with him to the highway and then turned back. I walked home by myself, slowly, feeling empty, and in those early years I accepted the fact that he could just walk away as mysteriously as he could appear in my life. I had seen them making love that morning before sunrise. Perhaps I had awakened that morning to the quiet sound of them trying to find some reason to stay together.

In those years I would say my prayers in English before I fell asleep, "Now I lay me down to sleep." I would bid my mother "good-night" in English. She never mentioned my father. If she missed him, she would not say, and I avoided talking about him. It was better just to say nothing and let my mother be. After I said my prayers, I tucked my hands under my throat to loosen my clothing and fell asleep, curled up against the wall. My brother slept behind me, next to Mom-mah, between the two of us who were his universe.

I remember the nights when I dreamed that those who were bigger and better were not so in my dreams and that I who was less than perfect had been perfect that day. When I fell asleep, more often than not I had nightmares. The worst nightmare came again and again. In that nightmare everyone spoke rapidly, and I could not understand what they were saying. They were looking at me and speaking, and as the speed of their speech increased, I became frozen with terror and could not move. When my mother heard me moaning, she would awaken me. "We inażį ksto," she would tell my younger brother, who stared at me wide-eyed— "Her blood stopped."

I know why my blood stopped. I remember the first time I encountered people like that in real life. They spoke rapidly, and everyone looked at me. My urge to run and hide under a bed increased until all I heard was the din of the voices in the kindergarten room where I stood on my first day. The din grew louder and louder, like rain falling on a tin roof. I panicked and thought that the noise would burst my ears and my equilibrium and I would fall with everything spinning faster and faster all around me. I felt nauseous and dizzy. The nights I had those dreams, I would lie for a moment with my head on the pillow, afraid to move.

I felt just that way when the kindergarten teacher and all the children looked at me on my first day at school in that small room in Nebraska, when I could not keep up with their excited voices that were speaking a language foreign to me. "Gar se bar dee, bar dee," I remember my younger brother saying when he wanted to play and pretend he was speaking English. One day he picked a bunch of dandelions and asked me, "Wat ese dis?" I shrugged, and he answered "flurs," and walked away proud of his English. Because it took me longer to answer correctly in English, I dreaded being addressed in that small classroom in Nebraska, and having all the children stare at me. I did not like their staring at me. It made me aware of how different I was, and it terrified me.

In the days before we moved to the reservation, on the day before school began, my brother, who was six years older than I and in the sixth grade, walked me to school and showed me the route we had to walk each day. Our house stood at the southeastern edge of town, on a dirt road back near the stockyards. We lived near other families like us, families who lived in small wood-frame houses that stood close together on two blocks or so of streets without sidewalks. Like the other houses, our house didn't have a lock on the front door, only a wooden peg about the size of a chalkboard eraser that kept the door from swinging open at night.

It was from that house that I first ventured forth to school. My older brother and I walked the eight blocks, winding across the railroad tracks, past the grain elevators, through the main street, and past the Chevrolet garage, the fire station, and the photography store, past the Lutheran church and up the hill to where the low-lying brick building stood. The building itself looked like any other small elementary school in Nebraska with its large windows and playground. How incredibly large the playground seemed to me as a small girl—a small Indian girl who would come out to play and find no one to play with but my own shadow.

It was a time when I looked forward to the loud siren from the nearby fire station announcing lunchtime. It kept track of time for me. When the siren blew at noon, I rushed out of the elementary school building and ran home for lunch. There at home I felt comforted by the sight of Mom-mah preparing lunch and by the sound of Lakota being spoken by her. "Wota ye!" she would say. "Eat!" I had a half hour to eat my lunch and return to school.

My lunch consisted of warm, sweet tea; a flatbread we called "oven bread" that was made out of flour, baking powder, cooking oil, and water; and fried "blo," or "potatoes." The potatoes came in large sacks. Our parents had picked them and in turn were paid with them by the growers.

I remember the potato fields in September, the month we call "Cȧwape ġi Wi," "the moon when the leaves turn brown." After the first frost killed the exposed part of the potato plant, the farmer plowed the fields, harvesting the potatoes. Mom-mah and others from the reservation followed behind the plow, picking the potatoes. They bent over the rows with sacks between their knees. The rough brown sacks hung from a wide belt that each picker wore. One sack hung half-open on two hooks on the front of the belt, and extra sacks hung from hooks on the sides and back. Each picker bent low to grab the potatoes with both hands and then threw them into the half-open sack hanging in the front. They were paid by the row.

I can still see Mom-mah as she bent low, moving the sack forward down the row as it got heavier and heavier. She always managed to pick fast and well, and the growers liked her. She was strong, and they said she was dependable. She never missed a day of work until the day one of the potatoes exploded in a fire they made to keep warm. The hot potato splattered on her as she stood warming herself by the fire. She showed me the small white scars on her legs where it had burned into her.

In early September, immediately after school let out, we hiked half a mile or so to the northeastern edge of town where the large potato fields were, to watch them pick potatoes. One day while I was watching, the farmer came by with his plow and exposed a mother field mouse to the elements. She ran with her babies attached and still nursing at her breasts. I felt sorry for her and her small pink babies who had no fur. I know many of the field mice

found shelter in the potato sacks Mom-mah and the others filled
and left at the edge of the picked rows. I would find the mice,
babies and all, in the full sacks they brought home.

I remember the day I was sick and stayed home from school. I
had pinkeye, and I couldn't go to school. In the old days it was
said that "Heyokʿa," the "clown," inflicted sore eyes and skin diseases on the people. In those days Heyokʿa was described as a
small man, old and mystical. He wore a cocked hat on his head,
carried a bow and arrows, and wore a quiver on his back. They
said that in winter he went naked and in summer wrapped himself in his buffalo robe. It must have been Heyokʿa who made my
eyes sore.

The grown-ups took me with them to work in the fields that
day, and I sat and watched an infant sleeping in a laundry basket
in Mom-mah's car. When the baby boy woke up, I ran into the
field where the pickers were to find his mother. She breast-fed
him, and he slept most of the day. Those were the days before we
left Nebraska forever and returned to the reservation. By the time
we moved, Mom-mah was older and could no longer bend down
to do the work of potato picking.

The day my older brother showed me the route to school, he
showed me a spot a block from school where the older kids ran off
through an alley toward the park and played all day. In that spot
they couldn't be seen, and they returned home only after school
ended. I remember one day that an older girl tried to pull me
along with her to the park, and my older brother played tug-of-
war with her until finally my brother, bigger and stronger than
she, pulled me away and off to school. My brother told me that
even when some of the older Indian kids, like the older girl who
had taken my hand, wanted to detour to the park, that I should
stick to the route and get to school on time.

I know that I listened to my older brother like a disciple, confused about the things he told me but wanting very much to be
like him. Sometimes he would reward me for listening, as on the
day he took his old white bike with only rims for tires and gave me

a lesson on it. He had named it "Casper." He walked to the empty side of a street with it, putting me in the seat, pushing me forward, and then running hard to keep up with me as I bumped down the dirt road, out of control, tipping to one side and then the other. I kept my hands on the handlebars and closed my eyes. My teeth chattered from the jarring of the wheels that had no rubber on them. He ran next to me, trying to keep me on course. Sometimes he would burst into loud laughter as I pulled ahead of him, my legs pumping vigorously. When he was finally convinced that I could ride the bike on my own, he gave it to me.

My brother then took a piece of cardboard from a box my mother used for carrying groceries and on that day, before school began for me, he used a new pencil to write my name on it. He said, "Caže okiwa yo," "yo" in the masculine voice, and handed me the cardboard. "Write your name this way," he had said. I looked at my brother with his hair cropped short, his new lace-up boots, and light-colored shirt tucked into his new jeans. My mother had taken us shopping for school clothes on Main Street that day, and my brother was wearing the shoes he would wear throughout the school year. He was older than me, and although we had older sisters, he took an interest in me and insisted that I pay attention to everything he had to teach me. "Maki pazo," we say in Lakota, and he would "show me," always ready to point out for me what he thought I should know. I was his pupil, sometimes begrudgingly so. I tried to write my name the way he showed me, but I couldn't, and soon he grew impatient and left me. When I wasn't my brother's pupil, I enjoyed being my younger brother's playmate. We played in the dirt with his small metal cars.

My mother had three sons, but I don't remember her oldest son at all as a child. He was older than me by more than a decade. I remember better my brother who was six years my senior. In my family I was in between my mother's two younger sons in age. They were the brothers I remember the best. These two brothers were different, like night and day, and I was able to benefit from their differences. My older brother wore his shirts ironed and his hair combed in the latest style. If no one said anything, my other brother, a year younger than me, could wear the same pair of jeans for weeks. His light brown hair hung over his eyes and seemed uncombed even when my mother hurriedly ran a comb through it.

My younger brother loved playing all sorts of games with whatever was at hand. His imagination took flight whenever he found a used kitchen match. He lined these matches up on the floor as armies preparing to go into battle. He would lie next to his matchstick armies, fighting great wars, making a nuisance of himself by protesting loudly whenever anyone disturbed his play. Sometimes he had so many matches lined up that no one could safely pass by him as he played on the floor. Mom-mah grew suspicious when he had too many matches. She suspected what I already knew was the truth. Instead of finding and playing with used matches, my brother would sneak into the large matchbox Mommah kept by the stove and light just enough matches to make it look as if they had been used for some legitimate purpose. In that way he enlarged his armies, fighting never-ending wars. When we played outdoors, my younger brother and I built elaborate roadways in the Nebraska dirt, and I mapped out houses and stores. Sometimes I would abandon our game and draw the insides of houses in the dirt with a large stick. I liked drawing living rooms with large picture windows, the kind I saw on my way to school.

My older brother by six years had a nervous twitch in his eye for awhile and took it upon himself to teach me correct English. He told me how to ask for a drink of water if I was thirsty: "May I have a drink of water, eya yo," he would say in the masculine voice—"Say it this way." He also taught me to say, "May I go to the bathroom?" He seemed insistent, and later I learned that a young Indian girl in his classroom had wet her pants because she was afraid to speak up in English. These were the first words that I learned in English, and I said one phrase more readily than the other.

I remember my mother standing at the corner near the drugstore, facing the street that led up a small incline to the school. She stood there waiting for me to be dismissed from a Girl Scout meeting for Bluebirds. She waited for me patiently, because it was getting dark and she worried about me walking home alone in the dusk. I could see her from a block away. She wore a black scarf wrapped around her shoulder-length hair and tied neatly at the chin. She wore a dark coat that was buttoned over a dark-blue cotton dress. She wore nylons and a pair of simple black shoes. She never wore slacks or skirts, only cotton dresses in darkflowered patterns. I have never seen my mother dressed in certain colors. She avoids orange, yellow, purple, green, and white. She avoids loud patterns, checks, or stripes. She avoids anything that brings attention to herself, yet her size commands attention. She is strong, and her large legs are not flabby. I have seen her take an apple in her hands and break it into two neat pieces.

I have grown up like her. I avoid the things she avoided, loud colors and prints, and I too pride myself in the strength of my legs to hold up the person I am and to someday hold up the person I want to be. I understand her more now, by looking back at those things that her mother must have cherished and those things which she too avoided. It is said that we Lakota "wįyą ke he na"— "were taught modesty and chastity." Had I lived as a young girl during my grandmother's time, I would have worn a chastity belt to protect my virginity and thus assure my position in the tribe as a chaste woman. I would have been a woman who lived according to the narrow but clear guidelines set by the elders, who believed that it is the woman who determines the future of the tribe.

I understand my mother more when I try to understand the way things were in the old days. I remember one picture, an old drawing by a Lakota man that depicted Lakota "wįyą," or "women in a group," standing shoulder to shoulder, watching a Sun Dance. They were all the same height, neither heavy nor too thin, all the same size. They stood with shawls wrapped around their shoulders and their long cloth dresses touching the tops of their moccasins. They were dressed in colors that were not bold like the colors men wore in the old days. The men dressed in reds, yellows, blacks, and whites. The women dressed in muted colors, like butterflies, in light blues and lavenders. They were dressed in simple prints and designs, like my mother. All thirteen women in the picture had dark hair that was parted down the center with two neat long braids falling over their breasts.

The way they wore their hair signified who they were. The hair parted down the center from the forehead back to the nape of the neck in one clear straight line and braided in one neat ropelike braid on each side of the head indicated self-knowledge: these women knew exactly who they were. Hair parted on the side and not down the center of the forehead, the way men sometimes did it, signified uncertainty. It said that the person who wears his or her hair that way was still seeking himself or herself. If one side of the hair was worn loose with the other side braided, it also signified that that person did not yet know himself or herself. Such people were usually men in the process of seeking themselves through dreams and visions.

We women seemed to know early on exactly what role was ours, and we sought only to perpetuate life unselfishly, if at all possible. If our braids were worn hanging to the back, it signified that we were single and available for marriage. Wearing our braids to the front, over the breast as in the Lakota artist's drawing of the women, signified that we were married and unavailable. Wearing our hair loose, down the backs, and unbraided meant that we were in mourning.

It is the way I prefer to wear my hair—loose, down my back, and unbraided—to signify that I am in mourning for everyone— my brother, my sisters, my grandfathers, my grandmothers, aunts, uncles, cousins, and all who have died before me and for everything that is dying before me. My mother, Le Ina mitąwa kį e, that mother of mine, is the only one who continues to live and seems to be the only one who understands why I wear my hair the way I do.

Wịyą Nupa, Double Woman

Mom-mah said in the old days that instead of scolding their children if they were misbehaving, mothers told them stories about Anuk Ite Wị, the Wịyą Nupa or "Double Woman." In referring to Double Woman, Mom-mah would say "Wịyą Nupa peka," in the old way. "Wịyą Nupa" is part of our origin or creation stories. Through these stories we learned that in the beginning, before the world and time, there was only consciousness. We learned that consciousness became aware of itself and its loneliness. It found itself lacking and wanted to create something to fill that void, something over which it could exercise its power and thereby feel fulfilled. Thus it created life.

It created Ịyą, "the Stone or Rock," who was all powerful. Ịyą, in turn, created Makạ, "the Earth and everything upon it," including Tᶜate, "the Wind," and Wakịyą, "the Thunder Being." Ịyą also created Ạpetu Wi, "the Sun," and Hạhepi Wi, "the Moon." He created Skan, "the Sky." It was said that Ịyą had two sons—Ksa, meaning "wise," and Iya, meaning "to speak." It is Ksa who later became known in our stories as Iktomi, the "Spider," the Trickster who was "witko," or "foolish"; Iya committed incest with his mother, who bore him a child called Gnaśkị ya, which means "insane." It was Iya who inflicted headaches and paralysis on people, just as Heyokᶜa inflicted sore eyes and skin diseases on them.

It was said that these stories were "woyake," meaning "spoken-it-is," and they were told so that our Lakota ways would be retained from one generation to the next. It took me a long time to understand these stories that were told to me in Lakota words spoken the old way. Perhaps for the same reason, it took me longer to understand the English language. It was this shifting from Lakota to English and back again throughout my childhood that prevented me from fully embracing one language or the other.

I grew up in a home without books. For the first few years of my life I do not recall seeing a book, except the small Bible Mommah kept in her purse. I grew up, not with books written in a language foreign to me, to Mom-mah, and to my maternal grandfather, Kah-kah, but with people around me: aunts, uncles, cousins, grandfathers, grandmothers, great aunts, and great uncles. They were my books. They told me stories in Lakota that I will never forget. Their own lives became stories that I will remember and will share with my children and their children.

In a world where only Lakota was spoken, I first became aware and conscious at the age of five. I became fully aware and began to rely on my own perceptions sometime after the age of eight, long after I had been exposed to the English language and its many nuances. It was at about eight years of age that I first remembered Mom-mah's stories. It was then that the idea of fear, as I know it now in English, entered my mind. In the ways of the Lakota, being fearful was not encouraged, but I felt fear anyway. Fear was the reason why I did not always like to hear these stories, to think the thoughts my ancestors had thought through these old stories told in the old words. I did not understand as a child and was afraid of them. I did not comprehend them until later in my life.

As a child I thought about our creation stories and tried to understand how "in the beginning" there was only consciousness. I tried to imagine what it must have been like when those stories were told in the old way, when only Lakota was spoken. I tried to imagine it as I lay next to my aunt, in her bed, under the warm covers, and listened to her tell me these stories in Lakota. In the darkness I was aware only of her voice. My imagination followed the light that her spoken words invoked in me. There in her warm bed I was not afraid. Her gentle and bemused Lakota voice would often lull me to sleep. There on her soft pillow I thought I could see what Iktomi, the "fool," looked like with his belly hanging low to the ground. It was then that I found a quiet place in my mind where I began to let go of my fear.

It was not until I was an adolescent and experienced my first purification ceremony in the "inipi," or "sweat lodge," that I was able finally to understand our creation stories and our Lakota belief regarding our collective consciousness. It was in the inipi, that round, small hut made of willow branches and covered with thick blankets, that I entered the womb of time and felt whole. It was there in the darkness that I finally understood Lakota consciousness, without light, shape, or form. I heard the voices of women—like Mom-mah at different stages of her life—young, middle-aged, and old—all crying, praying, and singing in the sweat lodge. In the darkness, I lost track of where the voices were coming from. When I emerged from that place, I realized those voices lived in me, that I lived in them. I heard them imploring Taku Śką Śką for "wiconi" or "life." Wiconi, for themselves, their children and families, brothers and husbands, and for all of their relatives, and I understood. I understood because I wanted wiconi for them and for all that was theirs; and whatever I had cried, prayed, and sang about in the inipi, they wanted for me. That is what Lakota consciousness was, and is, and even as a young girl, I understood.

It is in our creation stories that the Anuk Ite Wį or Double Woman first appeared. My grandfather, Kah-kah, said that Taku Śką Śką created man and called him "Pte Oyate." "Pte" is the name for the female buffalo, and "oyate" means "the people." Kah-kah said the first leader of the Pte Oyate was Wa, whose name means "snow," and his wife, Kal, whose name means "there." Their daughter, a beautiful girl, was named Ite, meaning "face." It is she who later became the dreaded Anuk Ite Wį or Wįyą Nupa.

It was said that Ite was beautiful and vain. She became the wife of Tᶜate, "the Wind," and gave birth to four sons. Their sons became the four sacred directions: west, north, east, and south. Her parents and the sons of Įyą encouraged her to seduce Ąpetu Wi, "the Sun." They hoped to gain immortality if she succeeded in seducing him. Since Ąpetu Wi was already the companion of Hąhepi Wi, "the Moon," its seduction of Ąpetu Wi was considered heartless. It was said that she broke the heart of her husband, Tᶜate, and that of Hąhepi Wi, who hid her face in shame. It is said that this is why the Hąhepi Wi goes through the different phases during the month, because she hides her face in shame.

When Ite seduced Ąpetu Wi, it was said that Skan, "the Sky," the judge of all things, saw what she had done and punished her by giving her a second face with grotesque features. Her two faces, one beautiful and the other hideous, became symbols of harmony and dissension. Her name became Anuk Ite Wį, the Wįyą Nupa. As further punishment, her unborn son was taken from her and became "Tᶜate Wam.niom.ni," which means "whirlwind." Wam.niom.ni is not one of the four sacred directions. It is, instead, that little whirlwind that blows by and then in confusion attacks itself, vanishing whence it came, from nothingness. When it blows by you, you might be tempted to say, "Takų he?" or "What is it?" In answer, a Lakota would say "tak ni śni," or "nothing."

In our culture, children are the most precious of all beings. They are called "wakᶜąyeża." The first part of the word, "wakᶜą," means "sacred or divine." To parents who raise their children in the old way, children are indeed sacred. It was said that when the missionaries saw the way we reared our children, they were appalled and called our child-rearing ways lenient. They wanted to take our children from us, and they did. When I look at my daughters today and imagine anyone thinking that they can take them from me, I die inside at the possibility, even the thought that someone who could never know or love them the way I do could take them from me. In the days when the government first put us on reservations, it sometimes succeeded in taking our children

away from us. Many children died in schools where they were be-
nignly neglected or abused. I know that many mothers and fathers
died inside when they took them away.

The missionaries and others outside the family did not understand that our children are all that is good in our hearts, our connection to all that is wak'ą. We know that all we bestow upon
them, life will bestow back on us. Our children represent our
Creator's trust in us. Through them we are able to see into the
seventh generation beyond the present. Outsiders did not know
our Lakota ways or understand even the most universal of all
laws that governed everything we did, the law of cause and effect.
We understood that the way we treat our children is the way life
treats us.

The way my mother told the story about Anuk Ite Wį or Wįyą
Nupa whenever my younger brother or I misbehaved was that in
the old days when children were acting the way we were—"wit-
kotkoka pi cayą," meaning "crazy-they-were-being," they were
told that they would be put outside for a few minutes to calm
them down. Outside the door stood Wįyą Nupa, who would
gladly take these children and snatch them away. The terrible
thing about Wįyą Nupa was that she had two faces, one beautiful
and the other hideous. Her beautiful face would soothe the child
while her hideous face would terrify her or him. Mom-mah said
that with one hand Anuk Ite Wį would calm the child, while with
the other hand she would spank the child with a "cąsaka la," or
"switch." Any child who heard the story the way Mom-mah told
it did not wish for the horrible fate that awaited them outside the
door and would instantly behave in a more appropriate manner. I
still feel that sense of fascination and horror when I hear the story
about Wįyą Nupa. Sometimes I think I understand the great wisdom behind the story about the beautiful and horrible creature:
she represents those two aspects of ourselves.

I grew up among many children—brothers, sisters, cousins,
and friends. I can see why our creation stories were told the way
they were. As children, we grew up conscious and aware of our

world, but it was not until we were able to speak fluently that we could express our thoughts and feelings about what it meant to grow up in a culture where children are sacred. It was partially our inability to speak as infants that made us sacred as children. Even when we could not speak, the elders in our midst seemed to know which children were "ksape" or "conscious, observant, and intelligent," by looking into our eyes. I remember Mom-mah saying "ksape la" when she saw my daughter as an infant. So, even a baby is conscious, observant, and intelligent in the Lakota sense.

We were never physically punished, nor were we yelled at or ridiculed by adults. They interacted among themselves, and we were expected to observe, listen, and learn the proper behavior. Mom-mah said that in the old days, girls became the responsibility of the mother and boys the responsibility of the father. When she was a young girl, her mother kept her near her and taught her what she needed to know. In the same way, she tried to keep me near her. When she had time, she would teach me those things she must have learned from her mother. "Wo mici gni," she would say, meaning "food-I-was-seeking," because much of Mom-mah's time was spent gathering resources for our use. I remember her hands, how busy they were, constantly cooking, cleaning, washing, mending, baking, combing hair, or counting change. I remember the way she kneaded bread: her strong knuckles pushed the dough flat on the pan before she baked it. My favorite "aġuyapi," or "bread," was her "oven bread." She baked in an oven she heated with wood from the woodpile. When we camped annually at the Sun Dance in August, she also made "wigli ų kaġapi," or "bread fried in oil in a skillet on an open fire." I preferred her oven bread, which always came out thick and warm.

I grew up like Mom-mah. I grew up without ever being struck by an adult. I have heard that other tribes treat their children this way. "Children are 'p'ąp'ą la,'" Mom-mah would say, "'delicate' or 'soft,' like the softest deerskin." Mom-mah has a gentle heart, and I have inherited it. As I grew older she would remind me of this when she wanted to teach me something: "Hecel inicaġapi śni," she would say. "You were not raised that way," meaning the way some children are raised, in a harsh way. She believed, as I now believe, that children learn best when they are raised in a gentle way. They said that when the tribes on the East Coast saw the European women strike their children, it horrified them. Why would you strike something sacred?

Mom-mah told us that when she heard a child cry in distress or pain she would say, "Tomakca kte sele," meaning "it makes me feel faint and sick." In the same way, I have a low tolerance when I hear a child crying. Mom-mah discouraged us from crying as we grew older. By the time I was ten, she told me that since I was getting older, it seemed particularly sad when I cried. When she told me that, it made me stop and listen. I heard myself crying, and I agreed with her. Mom-mah was raised by parents who remembered the old ways, perhaps the way Crazy Horse, Sitting Bull, and our great leaders were raised, by gentle and patient hands. I have heard stories told by men and women raised by their Lakota grandparents, who say their gentleness was like their soft old skin. How comforting it was to be loved that way.

Kah-kah said that when a child is born, he or she is given two sets of parents. The natural parents' roles are those of patient teachers. The appointed second parents, usually an aunt and uncle, had the roles of critical teachers who pointed out the child's wrongdoing and were the only ones who could actually scold the child. In those days, if a child engaged in deviant behavior, he or she was warned, "Taku ca oyale he ci iyeyąuį kte," meaning "Whatever it is you are seeking (through your behavior), you will find—good or bad." We lived in a world where words were heeded. The young listened to their elders, and the elders tried to live according to what they wished to teach. In those days everyone was a teacher, but only the young were allowed to make mistakes and learn from them. It was important that they be taught right. Even today Mom-mah says, "Tąyą ųspe śni ca he ų" whenever anyone makes a mistake, meaning "They did not learn properly, that is why."

When children like us were told stories, we learned to listen. We learned to obey and to respect the spoken word. We learned to keep quiet and observe. That was the way Mom-mah hoped I would always be when she had my ears pierced so that I would be an obedient child and in my obedience keep all that was Lakota alive in my heart. Mom-mah valued courage and would say "Wa kʻokpe śni ye," in the feminine voice. "Do not be fearful." She valued generosity and would tell me "Wateħla śni," meaning "Do not hoard things." She valued industriousness and abhorred laziness. She would tell us "Taku hena ableza ye, taku ociciyake hena," which meant "Try to see clearly the things I tell you."

It was thought that those who did not learn properly were "wicaśaśni," which literally translated means "Man-he-is-not." It meant that that person was devious, corrupt, or lacked character. It was a shameful word. I tried hard to learn properly, even when I was self-conscious and was only trying to learn in order to please Mom-mah. Like any child, I also had another voice inside of me—a voice that seemed to want the opposite of what Mom-mah wanted for me. I was a good listener and observer, but I was not a good and obedient child. I took everything to the extreme and even twisted it around. I learned to be too quiet and to question what others did by watching and guessing their intentions and discounting their actions. I was courageous but in an inconsistent way. I was generous but, as Mom-mah said, in a haphazard way. I was industrious but to the extreme. I was like the ant in the ant pile, carrying home useless beads for the joy of carrying something burdensome on my back. I was like the old woman who Mom-mah said sent her grandson back to a house where they had been overnight guests, to tell their hosts that it was not the grandmother who had released some stomach gas into the air the night they spent there. The grandson went back to the hosts and said, "ųci," meaning "grandma," "said to tell you that when she made noises with her behind, it really was not her." I thought too much and thought others did, too. I felt that sometimes I could see through others and they through me. I heard myself clearly pointing out my own imperfections to myself. I tried to be the perfect child like my older brother, but I often ended up being more like my mother than she or I realized. Perhaps she saw it. I did not.

I remember the woman who struck her small children out of frustration. Her whole life had broken down. Her mother had died, her father had remarried, and she herself had just turned twenty. Her new husband had left her with two small children. She had no one to help her, nothing to fall back on. She had no education or skill. Her only grace was a beauty that had turned from vibrant youth to pudgy middle-age by the time she had had her second child. I remember her because she struck her children. She was the closest one to what I had pictured the Anuk Ite Wị to be. She was outwardly a pleasant person to everyone but her small children. She seemed decent and caring in the way she washed them, combed their hair, and dressed them, but when she felt frustrated, something seemed to emerge from deep within her, something that terrified all of us who saw her strike her little children.

I remember standing next to Mom-mah on the day I watched the woman's son jump in pain as the woman struck him. I instinctively moved closer to Mom-mah, feeling her warm arm against me. I wanted Mom-mah to wrap those strong arms around me so that I could hide my face in her lap, but she didn't. Mom-mah sat rigidly and did not move. I did not move. I was rooted to the spot I felt was safe enough and far enough from the woman. Her son, a toddler, had nowhere to run, no one to turn to. I remember seeing the rage in his mother's eyes while her pretty pudgy face looked stony and cold. She struck her son while she held his elbow so he couldn't run and struck him over and over on the back side. She was silent, but I heard her rage. It sounded like an old 45 RPM record playing on slow speed. I heard it and tried to move under my mother's arm, but there was nowhere to hide. I felt her rage as I continued to stare at what she was doing, unable to take my eyes away from that small boy. I saw him jump in pain, and I felt her rage sting my face and my eyes as if she had struck me. Mom-mah must have felt me feeling that small boy's pain, for she said to me,

"H̊eyabeyayaye." It meant, "Get away. She thinks that she can get a reaction from me." I ran away, behind her, but I could not run from the image of that child hopping in pain. I know that that day I saw the Anuk Ite Wį.

I remember that day, and I feel that same dread and horror I felt when I thought my mother was going to put me out the door where the Anuk Ite Wį would snatch me away. When I look back, I know that that woman who beat her small son would have done better if she could have, if she had known a better way, but by the time she had her children, the old ways were disappearing and she had forgotten that we Lakota never strike our children. I still try to imagine what I would have done had I been bigger as I stood next to my mother, how I would have, if I had been bigger, intervened for that "wakˈąyeża," that "sacred little being." I remember hearing the news that someone in Nebraska had taken that little boy and put him in a foster home along with the other little child the woman had had, and I was glad. I was glad that wherever he was, I knew the Wįyą Nupa wouldn't find him, because she lived next door to us.

Weighed Down by Buckskin

In August in Nebraska, all the farmers and ranchers come into town for the county fair. There is a parade on Main Street and a rodeo and carnival at the county fairgrounds. The fairgrounds sit at the edge of town, at the eastern end next to the cornfields where the paved road ends and the gravel roads begin. The rodeo is the main event at the fair. A small carnival traveling through provides entertainment for everyone. The usual Ferris wheel, rides, and sideshows accompany the carnival. One year a carnival brought a hippopotamus in a trailer, and people paid a quarter to see it open its wide jaws. I remember my mother standing on the narrow step, peeking into the trailer and then falling back when the hippopotamus opened its mouth.

I also remember one August, during the month we call "Wasut'ų Wi," or "the moon the chokecherry ripens," the temperature was about ninety degrees. I stood behind the drugstore on Main Street. My mother left me there to wait while she checked on the progress of the parade. I was supposed to be in the parade as part of an Indian dance group, but we were late and the parade had already started. Mom-mah left me on the sidewalk, and I stood next to where she left my buckskin dress in a bag. My hair, neatly combed into two long braids, fell down my back. My braids were tied securely close to my ears with two beaded hair ties decorated with feathers. When I moved, the bright feathers fluttered lightly like cotton candy.

I wore a boy's white T-shirt, jeans, buckskin leggings, and a pair of beaded moccasins. My cheeks were brushed with rouge, and I wore a beaded headband across my small forehead. I felt hot and sweaty. I had seen my father select the bolt of buckskin at the arts and crafts store on the reservation. He had bought another outfit for me at the same time he bought the buckskin. In the old days he would have had to kill an elk to make a dress for me. They said it took one whole elk for a small girl's dress. He also bought two "fancy dance" boys' costumes for my older brother. The other outfit I owned was not buckskin but was made of dark blue, blanketlike material. It felt lighter and easier to wear. It had several bands of bright red-and-white ribbon sewn around the collar, hem, and cuffs. It was my favorite dress. It had small ivory-colored shells or simulated elk's teeth all up and down the front, about seven rows each of eight or nine teeth. It had matching leggings, and I wore the same moccasins I wore with my buckskin dress. I preferred the blue blanket dress to the buckskin one, especially in August when the high temperatures and dry weather meant that everything was covered by a light powder of fine, dry dust.

The day I stood on the sidewalk behind the drugstore, I held an ice cream cone in my right hand, a double scoop of chocolate chip that came from the counter at the soda fountain. In all the years we ordered ice cream from that drugstore, we never sat at the counter. We usually ordered and then took our purchases with us, out the door to our side of town. That day as I stood quietly licking my beloved treat, a little white girl, a "wasicu," looked at me standing in my boy's white T-shirt, jeans, and headband and said, "Look Mom, a little Indian boy." I continued to lick my cone that was melting in the heat and quietly watched her. I thought it preposterous that she would call me an "Indian boy," but I did not challenge her assertion. I just waited for her to go away so that I could eat my ice cream cone in peace.

In those days we did not converse with the wasicu. We were too self-conscious in our use of English, and they were too self-conscious to speak to a Lakota. The only people who spoke to us

were the storekeepers, and they raised their voices an octave as if
we were hard of hearing. "How are you doing?" they would yell,
not waiting for an answer. "Okay," my mother would yell back.
"Toṡke . . . ma nųḣcą kecį se ce," she would add. "Does he think
I am deaf?" Mom-mah loved to make side comments in Lakota
when she spoke to the merchants on Main Street. "How much do
you want for that?" she would ask, pointing to an object for sale.
"Four dollars," the merchant would say, or "maza ską topa,"
meaning "four of the white metal," which signified money or
dollars. Mom-mah would say under her breath, "Zigzica na ṡice
eyaṡ," which meant, "It is flimsy and poorly made. Why ask that
much for it?" My mother would then walk away, and the merchant might say, "I'll tell you what. I'll give it to you for two and
a half bucks." "I'll take it," my mother would say, money in hand.
I do not remember any real conversations between us and them,
only an exchange of money and goods. The money was worth far
more than the cheap goods we bought at premium prices. It was
in this place that I learned to grow quiet and to watch the waṡicu
with distrustful eyes—the way the storekeeper watched me when
I entered his store on Main Street.

When I put on my buckskin, my bright beads, and my moccasins, suddenly the waṡicu shed his distrust and paid me quarters to
pose with me for photographs. I know how Sitting Bull must have
felt when they wanted to pose with him. I saw my pictures from
those days, a somber-faced little girl in buckskin and feathers, my
forehead wrinkled in a hot frown. I was not a smiler; smiles did
not become me. I was a frowner from the beginning. I frowned in
more pictures than I can remember so that by the age of thirty my
forehead should have resembled a plowed field with neat, even-
spaced rows of deep frowns acquired over a lifetime of practice.

I wore my buckskin dress at the age of seven, even when I did
not want to wear it. When I put it on for the county fair in August,
it felt hot and heavy. My whole outfit consisted of the buckskin
dress, buckskin leggings, beaded moccasins, a beaded headband,
beaded hair ties with bright-colored feathers, and a long bone

necklace that covered my entire chest. The bone necklace I wore was actually simulated bone. It made a lot of noise when I moved, so I did not move much. It sounded like rocks rattling in a cardboard box, and when I felt hot and uncomfortable, the noise irritated me. I felt too weighed down when I was dressed in my full buckskin outfit—heavy and painfully self-conscious.

I danced the traditional women's dance, which required that I stand in one spot and move my knees up and down to the rhythm of the drum. I could dance in a circle in the spot I stood, but once I planted myself I did not move. If I did move, I walked in a direction opposite the men, tiptoeing and jerking my knees to the beat of the drum. We all danced in a circle—men, women, and children. The men and boys danced in one direction in a circle to the right, and the women and girls danced in the other direction in a circle to the left. Women danced on the outside, enclosing the men in the inner circle. The role of women was to be on the outside, as spectator, even while dancing. We watched our men who watched themselves dancing.

My brother's two outfits were different from the traditional outfits in that they were more feathery and showy. My older brother wore his outfit less self-consciously. He danced tall and proud, his light skin glistening in the heat. He looked slender and light in his outfit. He wore four sets of round feather bustles, one on his upper back, one on his lower back, and two smaller ones on his shoulders. He wore a headgear called a roach that was made out of porcupine hair. He also wore a beaded headband with three small mirrors fastened to it, one on the front and two small ones fastened to each side. These small mirrors caught the reflection of the bright sun and flashed back brilliant light when he moved his head.

He wore beaded cuffs and a beaded belt over a loin cloth. He wore shaggy leg gear with bells tied at the ankles and beaded moccasins. He lifted his legs high, dancing lightly, and deliberately moving sometimes like a bird spreading its wings and twirling in time to the rhythm of the drum. When I see a hawk or eagle circling lazily in the sky, I remember my brother spreading his thin arms wide in a circle as he danced around and around. His only limitation was the drum. When it stopped, he too had to stop at the last beat or the other dancers would give a loud cry of dismay and the older men would say he missed it. "Naśna. Hą-ų . . . hą-ų," they would say, meaning, "He missed it. Too bad, too bad." My brother was easily embarrassed and wanted to please the adults around him. He tried never to miss a beat. He could keep perfect rhythm to the drum. Being six years older than I was, he seemed much more capable.

I felt no joy in my dancing. I did not look forward to the heat and dust at the county fair. I could not say, "Wawaci kte śni," which means "Dance-I-prefer-not-to." Even the songs sung for us to dance to were meaningless. For me, it all came down to spectator versus me. I did not want to perform, to dance in my heavy buckskin dress in the dusty heat, to dance to the small sound of the drum. The drum competed with the loud sounds of the livestock at the rodeo. When I look back on those days, I know what Mom-mah meant when she would say to us, "Wacį t'ąka ye," which literally meant, "Enlarge your thoughts" or "Be patient" or "Show endurance." As a child, I tried to be that way, to endure in a long-suffering way, as only a child knows how to do when asked to do something against her will.

I danced with other men and women. We were all given payment in the form of free beef. We had to appear at the appointed time and place in the center of the rodeo arena where I had seen the "Heyok'a," or rodeo "clown," run and hide in a wooden barrel. The clown ran and hid there to try to distract the massive bull that the riders rode in the rodeo. When the rider was thrown from the bull, the Heyok'a ran into the arena frantically waving red flags and diving into the barrel, which the bull then attacked with a fury. Those times I stood in the arena, small and boiling under the dress, I felt the bull's rage. My insignificance enraged me. I was all buckskin dress, feathers, and regalia, fluttering in the heat. I was shriveling under that dress. And there was no barrel for me to dive into.

I stopped dancing when my buckskin and elk's teeth dress burned in a house fire. At least I stopped doing the kind of dancing I had done for the county fair and rodeo. I danced with my cousins and friends at summer powwows on the reservation where I no longer worried about the spectators, because they were my relatives, my "tiošpaye," my extended family. We called our powwows "wacipi," or "that place where they danced." At those dances we flung long cloth shawls upon our backs, over T-shirts and jeans. These shawls are called "šina kaswpi," "šina" meaning "shawl" and "kaswpi" referring to the long "fringes" decorating the cloth shawl. We wore our hair long and loose down our backs. Our faces expressionless, we danced in a line of twos, side by side with a partner. The older girls were usually in the front, the younger girls behind them. We danced as the men—my uncles and cousins dressed in bells and feathers, and usually in full regalia—danced in the opposite direction. The spectators would later tease us. They said that we danced with only one thing on our minds—boys. We danced intermittently, spending our time at the powwows looking at which-boys-stood-where and which-girls-were-with-which-boys. In our attraction to boys, we resembled the moths that flew around the high outdoor lights that lit the pine-covered dance arbor at night. We were like the "wanaǧi t'a kim mela," the "ghost butterfly," which is what we call the common moth.

The dancing on those summer nights, when the crickets sang by the creek and the lightning bugs flickered like dancing "wanaǧi," or "spirits along the water," was a natural part of me. On those cool evenings, the šina kaswpi on my shoulders felt right, and I danced unhurried and relaxed while the spectators sat in folding chairs around the pine arbor.

I wore moccasins, and my feet felt light upon the grass where the wacipi were held. I listened to the drummers so sure in their song. I listened to the bells ringing as my male relatives danced. I watched how the old women danced, swinging their šinas back and forth rhythmically. That was how I danced those nights when the announcer at the powwow called out, "Hokahe, hokahe, wacipi yo, wacipi yo, wacipi yo," which means, "Strengthen your hearts, be strong, dance, dance, dance."

Death Part 1

I was told I had a little sister, but she was sickly, my mother said. She died before I remember. I only remember crying later beside the old metal trash can where my mother burned all the things that belonged to my little sister. I remember gazing at the metal trash can, the fire brimming over the rim, and the smell of plastic burning. I was crying, not because I would miss a little sister that I didn't remember, but because my mother burned everything that had been hers. She did not spare one plastic baby bottle or nipple. I cried because I was attached to those bottles and nipples, even as old as I was at four. "Toške," my mother would gently chide me, "Why do you want them?" I remember finding comfort under the bed with my precious bottles, my cheek cradled on my arm, enjoying the dark, sucking contentedly on a plastic bottle filled with a mixture of warm tea and sugar. When my little sister died, she took with her my attachment to those bottles, and I cried loud and long.

I grew up with death all around me. It happened, and we children were not shielded from it. We were part of the funeral and mourning process. We peeked into the coffin and gazed at dead relatives who were on their way along the wanaǧi road, on their way down the "ghost or spirit road." This spirit road can be seen in the night sky if you look and find the Milky Way. That is our "spirit road" or "wanaǧi tą cąku," taking us home to the spirit world where all of our departed relatives are. "Mititakuye kį hiyo

ma hi pi na wicoti ekta amakį pi," my mother would say. "My
relatives from the spirit world came for me to take me home." She
has told me many times that they have come for her in dreams, but
always she tells them that it is not yet her time, that no one will
care for the children.

I was not afraid of death as a child. The first death I became
aware of was my little sister's. I saw death when a niece died in our
house the same way, mysteriously and without warning. They call
it Sudden Infant Death Syndrome now. I saw it one winter night
when we went to sleep with my niece, a six-month-old baby, in
our midst, loved and cuddled. The next morning we heard the
anguished cries of her mother and father, crying over her still
body, as mystified as we children were over what took her "nagi"
or "spirit" away. The baby had been alive the night before. "Ni
ų," meaning "alive it dwelled." The next day, the baby was "tʻe,"
"dead." My brother held his daughter in his arms, crying until
someone gently pried her away. I saw his tears and face imprinted
upon hers. I remembered my niece, fat and sleepy a few weeks
before, peacefully napping. She looked different in death. I remembered then how my mother had said not ever to take a picture
of a sleeping baby. "Wa wakųza," she said, meaning "If you take
a picture of a sleeping baby you might wish upon the sleeping
child a death wish." Mom-mah, like all Lakota, felt that our
thoughts can influence the outcome of any situation, and the
word "wakųza," meaning "to influence," was a very important
word. Whatever we did or thought should never influence in a
negative way the outcome of any situation. To Mom-mah, someone as sacred as a child should not be photographed while asleep.
I thought of that as I looked upon the baby who in her death slept
with a baby bonnet upon her head and a rattle in her hand.

The first funeral I became aware of was my older sister's. Mom-
mah and Kah-kah called my sister, who was my mother's oldest
child, by her Indian name, Keg-le or "Keg-lezela Wį," meaning
"Spotted Turtle Woman." It was Keg-le, eighteen years my senior,
to whom I was most attached of all my siblings. When she died, I

saw Mom-mah and her relatives, mostly women, burn her clothes, shoes, bedding, hair brushes, combs, and anything she wore or personally touched. They even burned her vanity case, which was made of a pale green vinyl and had a small mirror glued on the inside cover. How she loved to look into it while she pinned her dark hair into tiny pin curls. When the vinyl case burned, it smelled like an old tire burning. The women piled up Keg-le's things in a small clearing away from her house, poured kerosene on them, and set them ablaze with a kitchen match. They burned all of her belongings except for her photographs. These they gave to my mother.

She had a camera, a black box that you looked down into to focus. She loved taking pictures, making people pose while she gazed down at them through her lens, capturing their image on black-and-white film. There were very few pictures of her. She took many pictures of others, some of me frowning in my buck-skin dress, some of relatives who looked slimmer and younger and who have since traveled the "wanaġi" or "ghost" road. The pictures that she took of everyone else were what she left behind. She kept them in a round metal box, an old cracker tin that kept them dry and unwrinkled. It was her legacy, what she left, and what was later taken by a fire that destroyed Mom-mah's house. It was be-lieved that these photographs were Keg-le's and perhaps they, too, should have been burned.

When I saw the women going through Keg-le's things, and I saw the women that she had not liked when she was alive touch her things, I wanted to push them away. Keg-le had loved me as if I were her own child. When she died, I know a part of me that could not cope with the idea that she was gone forever shut itself down. I regress to that hurt part of me even now, and find myself seeking the company of older women who remind me of Keg-le, someone to fill that void she left when she died. I went everywhere with her, and often people thought we were mother and daughter.

In our eyes we were, Keg-le and I, a parent and child. Through some fluke of nature, she could not bear children. I became her surrogate child. Such things were permitted in our culture. We had ceremonies for such events. In the old days, if Keg-le wanted me as her daughter, she would have made me her daughter in the "huka lowąpi" ceremony where such things were done, "huka" meaning "relative" and "lowąpi" meaning "they sing." They sang for the right to call someone a relative. They said that the missionaries who had come were against this ceremony and had said it was wrong. Had we lived back then, Keg-le and I would have undergone the ceremony anyway, for even when they outlawed these ceremonies, we still had them quietly. Keg-le would have made me her daughter, and I would have honored her as a mother.

When I saw the women that Keg-le didn't like, going through her personal things after she died, I felt ashamed for not liking them, but I felt it anyway. I watched them carefully, the women she had not liked, to see if they would cry, to see if their tears were real. They stood quietly, dry-eyed, watching all that was left of Keg-le and her worldly possessions burn. In the old days it was said that when someone died and his or her spirit was making the journey to the spirit world, they were happiest when another spirit came along with them. For this reason, sometimes a man's horse or dog was slain and laid to rest next to him. Perhaps that is why they burned Keg-le's things, so that her spirit could take with it all the things it had in this world. Keg-le took care of her things. Mom-mah said that she did not want to give anything to someone who would not take care of her things the way Keg-le would have. "What about me?" I wanted to ask. It was the one question I had. It was a question which no one could answer because I could not ask it. I could not articulate my own grief. What was I going to do without her?

As children, we had to learn to deal with death by watching the adults around us. When someone in our family died, Mom-mah received all the attention, as if her grief were more important than anyone else's. I ignored my mother and the other grieving adults and grieved the only way I knew how, as a child. I played. Keg-le's wake lasted two nights, and on the third day she was buried. I

played at the wake with the children who came with their parents
to pay their last respects. I played until I was exhausted. I played
tag. I chased others, and they chased me until I was exhausted and
could no longer run. I ate as many slices of cake and pie as I
wanted. I ate when the adults ate, and I played while the wake
went on around me. I stayed up late, and some nights fell asleep
under a bench near Keg-le's coffin. All the while I was acutely
aware of Keg-le in her coffin. She lay there looking like someone
else, her unnaturally neat hair, her crisp new dress, and her skin
looking like someone dusted it with a fine powder. Her face was
made up, and they perched her glasses on her still face as if she
would need them where she was going.

My mother said, "Wakuze se ce," when Keg-le cut my hair a
few months before she died. "Maybe it is an omen." All of my life
I had had long hair that Keg-le had carefully washed and combed.
She trimmed my bangs and fixed them into a ponytail with some
of my long hair falling straight and down my back. She tirelessly
braided my hair at night and used a fine comb to keep it free of
lice and nits. She disliked anything unclean. She smelled of clean
things like floor cleaner, face cleaner, shampoo, and the lotions
which she used to keep my thin arms and legs from looking
chapped and dirty. "Takwe he-canu he?" Mom-mah asked. "Why
did you cut her hair?" When Keg-le cut it and curled it with a foul-
smelling permanent solution, my mother was puzzled. "Wakuze
se ce." Mom-mah told her to remember the old beliefs that say
you only cut your hair if someone close to you dies. So, when
Keg-le died, Mom-mah said that perhaps she had been preparing
for her own death. She must have known that she was dying, and
no one would take care of me as she had. That was why she had
cut my hair, the hair she loved.

It must have been true, what Mom-mah said. Keg-le was dying, and I was too young to see it even when it was happening. I
remember the trips I made with her to Main Street. Our Main
Street, two blocks long, had three liquor stores. It also had two
drugstores, a five-and-dime store, two clothing stores, a hardware

store, a Chevrolet dealership and repair garage, a grocery store, three restaurants, a barbershop, a justice of the peace, a grain and feed store, a bakery, a farm equipment dealer, and a theater. Keg-le did most of her shopping at the liquor store on Main Street, the one next to the Chevrolet dealer. We would walk into the store, which always seemed dark, regardless of the time of day, and we would leave immediately after she bought her small bottle of liquor. She carried her purchase in a small brown paper sack under her coat. "M.niśa," it is called, "red water." In the old days it was sometimes called "m.ni wak'ą" or "water that is divine or mysterious." Keg-le drank m.niśa as often as she could. I had seen her take a swig out of what she had in those small paper sacks. She would drink it and grimace as if in pain. Her throat seemed to constrict, and then she would hold the liquid in her mouth for a second and swallow it. I remember seeing others do the same, as if the m.niśa was being rejected by the throat and it took tremendous effort to force it down.

I had seen Keg-le's friends, women who loved to share her bottles of cheap wine, squatting by the stockyard. They squatted down to sneak a drink, in case the policeman was driving by. The policeman knew them all by their first names, even the blue-eyed one whose father had never claimed her, so that she lived among us speaking only our language, never learning to read or write in English. They passed around the small paper bag, drinking from the bottle after wiping the neck with their sleeves, their faces becoming flushed with a temporary glow. Among Keg-le's friends were women who sometimes fell on the railroad tracks, numb with alcohol, and could not move. "O t'e," we would say, "like dead." The women lay as if they were dead, perhaps seeking a reprieve, a brief moment of rest from the reality of what they had become. When they were not drinking, they were "nacaca"; that is, "their hands shook like dry sticks in the wind," and they shivered until they were able to get more of the red water.

I remember the two sisters who were Keg-le's favorite drinking friends. They loved to laugh, and they spent hours lying in the grass and talking at the public park. The three of them would meet at the park. Sometimes they would share a bottle of wine while I played on the playground with the daughter of one of Keg-le's good friends. The two sisters must have been attractive at one time, but when they were lying in the sun at the park, they looked dark and small. They had a fondness for raw lemons which they poured salt on and then ate, scraping the rind with their teeth. I played on the seesaw and the merry-go-round with the little girl whose mother died before Keg-le did. She was my favorite playmate. She loved to giggle at everyone and everything the same way I did. One day Keg-le and her friend decided to buy Easter dresses for us. The two drunk women took us to Main Street and bought the same lavender dress in two different sizes for us. I was taller than my friend and needed a size larger. I remember how delighted I was to put on that Easter dress and to see my friend in the exact same dress. How fun it was to look like twins for a day.

On our way home, my little friend and I admired the daffodils and buttercups that had bloomed before Easter, and we made plans to return to the park for the Easter egg hunt. Keg-le and her friends stumbled past the railroad tracks, walking behind us as we skipped along in our new Easter dresses. They tried hard to look sober. "Itom.ni se mani pe śni ye," Keg-le told her friends. "Try not to walk like you are drunk." As soon as my friend and I passed the railroad tracks on the way back to our neighborhood, one of Keg-le's friends, walking behind us, as if on cue tripped and fell upon the railroad tracks. We rushed back to help her up, her small daughter holding one elbow and her sister holding the other. Keg-le and I pushed her up from the back, trying to keep her upright. I remember giggling and then looking to see if my little friend was doing the same. I saw her trying to keep her tears back, and I became afraid for her. Her mother leaned against her, soiling her new Easter dress.

They all died, one by one: Keg-le's friends, the two sisters, and the others. I didn't see my little friend again until we moved to the reservation, where she lived with her grandmother. She had forgotten me, but I will never forget her mother, her aunt, and Keg-le. They died from the alcohol they drank every day, like water. I remember hearing somewhere that we humans are creatures of bread and wine. This saying must have been meant for Keg-le's friends, who lived more for the m.niśa than anything else. It was no surprise that after someone died and the group of women who drank by the stockyards grew smaller and smaller, the women began to hold their own memorial services for those among them who had friends or relatives that died. They would take their bottle of cheap wine and consecrate it, pouring a drop on the ground for each person who died. It was an act of true generosity, an act that required taking some of their beloved wine and pouring it into the wind. In the old days, it was thought that the "naġi," or "spirit nearby," would appreciate such a gesture of generosity. The ritual must have been held for Keg-le, who died far from home, far from her women friends, from the three liquor stores on Main Street, and from me.

According to Mom-mah, the "wanaġi mak'oce," or "spirit world," was a place where all of our deceased relatives are, a place where they lived with glad hearts, "cate waśteya." She said, "If you die drunk, your spirit will never find its way to the spirit world." I remember the small airplane that brought Keg-le home from Omaha, where she had died. I saw it skip down the small runway and come to a stop near where Mom-mah and I stood along with other relatives. We had waited for the plane all morning, running back and forth between the hangar and where our car was parked. We waited until someone said, "Wana ku welo," meaning, "Now-he-comes-home," referring to the plane as if it were a person on its way to where we stood waiting for Keg-le's body. In the old days, if someone said "wana ku welo," he might be referring to a scout that was bringing news. For me, the plane verified the news that Keg-le did, in fact, die. With death all around me, as a child I sometimes did not, or perhaps refused to, believe that someone actually died until I saw that person's body in a casket.

I saw them lift Keg-le out of the plane on a stretcher. She was entirely covered by a white cloth. Nothing of her showed. They loaded her into the back of a long black car that belonged to the undertaker who was to prepare her for burial. We followed the undertaker back through town and watched him drive on through to the next town where the funeral home was. I remember the day they summoned my mother to the appliance store on Main Street where she took her telephone calls. The hospital in Omaha called to tell my mother, Keg-le's next of kin, that Keg-le had died. Her liver had stopped functioning. There was nothing anyone could do. I remember my mother sitting at the kitchen table, numb and still. "Cųkśi, toki la le kį t'ąį śni," she finally said when she began to cry. "Daughter, where are you?"

I was glad Keg-le didn't die drunk. She died in a hospital room somewhere in Omaha, my mother said. Had she died drunk, her naǧi or spirit would forever roam the earth like T'ate Wam.niom.ni, the little whirlwind, that lost soul who is Anuk Ite Wį's unborn child. The little whirlwind blows by and throws dust in your eyes, hoping to get your attention so that you will feel sorry for it. Perhaps, if you feel so inclined, you will take your bottle of m.niśa and spill a drop on the ground for it.

Death Part 2

The things I understood about death came from my grandfather, Kah-kah, and my mother, "Ina," or as I called her, "Mom-mah." When someone died, either Kah-kah or Mom-mah would tell my brothers and me about "naġi," the spirit. In earlier times, before it was against the law to practice our old rituals, it was common to perform a Keeping-of-the-Soul ceremony when someone died. In that ceremony, an individual close to the dead person would pledge to keep and to guard the spirit of the dead person for one "waniyetu" or winter. When they said it was unlawful to practice our old rituals, we did them anyway and called them something else. When I was growing up, we had "memorial giveaways," which were really a modified Keeping-of-the-Soul ceremony. In that ceremony we did everything except that part which offended the Christians.

I remember being afraid of "wanaġi," or what I thought were "ghosts," but Kah-kah said naġi are everywhere and to not be afraid because I had a naġi who protected me. He said that anything that had been alive, "ni ų," or had been a part of life, "woniya," had a spirit that was part of the divine or "wak'ą" and should be respected and treated as what it was, sacred. I was afraid when anyone said "wanaġi," for I remembered how my older brother said he had seen one. He said he heard a knock at the front door one night, and when he went to answer it, no one was there but a wanaġi. It scared him so that he developed a nervous twitch in his right eye, and for a while he seemed to wink continually at everyone. One day his twitch went away on its own. I was afraid and thought I would be next. So whenever anyone knocked at the door and I was home alone, I wouldn't answer it. I would hide under the bed, in the dark, rather than risk seeing something that wasn't there.

Kah-kah said the spirits of animals are called "wamak'a naġi." When I was little, I was afraid of them, too; back then everything was mysterious and divine. I remember a dead bobcat in a tree near the edge of town. Seeing its decomposing body wedged between two high branches, I became afraid of it. Kah-kah said that everyone is afraid of bobcats, dead or alive. The "igmu," or "cat," is an animal that is not eaten. When it dies, it is left alone, because if anyone touches it, that person will be "napṡupsu"—become palsied or crippled in some way.

Mom-mah said that when a person dies, like my oldest sister Keg-le, her naġi is nearby for a while. So during the few days of her wake and funeral we all had to be careful in what we said and did. Mom-mah said that whatever way we were being during that time, good or bad, would be the way we would remain. I tried hard to be good. I wanted people to say, "He wicicala ki waṡtela," or "she is a good girl," during the wake and funeral, but often I forgot and I played too much. I wanted to make new friends. I wanted to eat sweet things and share them with my new friends. I forgot my mother during those few days. I knew whatever Mom-mah told us was right. "Lena hecetu ḣca slolwaye," she would say. "I know these things are so." Mom-mah must have been right. I became what I was during Keg-le's funeral, because even today I am still seeking the friends I did not make. I am still a lover of sweet things to eat, and I have forgotten many times that Mom-mah is not the benevolent naġi I remember her to be, but rather a human being capable of selfishness and even error.

She set aside her grief when Keg-le died and busied herself with all the details of the wake and funeral. Like in an Emily Dickinson poem, she swept up the debris left by death and attended to the practical things. When Keg-le died, Mom-mah went to the rendering plant nearby and bought a whole cow, freshly slaughtered, to feed all the people who came to the wake and funeral. They brought the cow and left it next to an outdoor water pump, where we drew our drinking water. There they used the water from the pump to rinse and soak the freshly butchered meat. My mother and her friends and relatives grabbed large kitchen knives and headed for the carcass, knives clinking against a sharpener. The women gathered around the cow, and the butchering began outward from a place on the skin next to the stomach. A straight line was slashed and the fur peeled back. Their knives went quickly to work. A woman gathered the skin in one hand like folds in a blanket. She held the skin back, fold by fold, and skinned the animal with the knife that was in her other hand. She skinned the animal from the stomach out. How easy she made it look, her knife glistening in the morning sun, sweat springing to her brow.

I remember that once I saw a vision in the heart of a thunderstorm. The thunder roared like nothing I had ever heard. In my vision I saw Lakota women running in traditional buckskin dress, with beaded encasements for the knives that were hanging from the belts of their dresses. They ran as only women with legs hindered by their long dresses can run. They rushed upon a felled buffalo bull, wounded but alive. They pulled their knives in unison from their sheaths and swiftly skinned the animal. All the while the buffalo bellowed, incensed and wild. Its bellow was the sound of the thunder cracking overhead, and their knives became the lightning that flashed across the sky. In my vision I saw the women in the heat of the thunderstorm with sweat upon their brows, knives flashing, their faces intent upon the kill.

It was like that—Mom-mah and the women butchering that cow. "Swish, swish, swish" went their knives. "Thud, thud, thud" went the axes they used to break the bones for the sweet white marrow inside. Some of the women cut into the innards of the cow, called the "t'aniġa," to get the intestines, heart, liver, kidneys, and the inner lining of the stomach. The kidney is a delicacy that is washed and eaten raw with salt sprinkled on it. It is cut into bite-sized pieces and passed around among the women. A piece of the fat surrounding the kidney is also sliced and passed along with the kidney. Everyone takes one bite of each, savoring the raw taste of fresh kidney. Mom-mah taught me never to refuse food that is offered to me. "Wašte nicila kecįpi kte," she said. "They will think you hold yourself above them, that you think you are better than they are." So, I accept humbly what is offered to me. I have tasted everything, including t'aniġa when it is washed and boiled into a grayish-looking soup.

The women bring metal tubs and buckets and fill them with water. In these containers they throw the cow's intestines, which are called "t'ašupa" and are delicious fried or boiled. They work long and hard, turning everything from the cow into something edible and good, as in the old days when our lives centered on the buffalo hunt. "T'aniġa," my mother calls it, all the "innards" of the cow, which she enjoys as a delicacy. It is only on special occasions that she purchases a cow, or even the t'aniġa that the rendering plant will sell to her.

One of the older women who was butchering the cow said, "Wap'ata pi ca taya s'ele" to Mom-mah, who nodded "ha," meaning "yes." "Butchering makes everything seem fine, again," said the woman to my mother. My mother agreed. In the old days our lives revolved around such times, when the buffalo was the center of our universe. The t'at'aka, that great sacred animal. The buffalo back then was considered a gift from T'ųkašila, and in humble gratitude, everything that came from it was used, nothing wasted.

The women work together until everything is soaking in cold salt water or is being cut into pieces the size of a fist for stews to feed the people. Stews consist of meat, potatoes, cabbage, carrots, and celery. In the old days the stews would be of buffalo meat that was cut into fist-sized pieces and combined with wild turnips called "tıpsila." I do not like tıpsila, but I do like potatoes and cabbage. Mom-mah encourages the women to take some of the extra t'aniġa home, and they fill empty five-pound coffee cans with the grayish-looking lumps, including the intestines and inner lining of the stomach. The dogs are the last to enjoy the "wap'ata" or "butchering": they are thrown the large bones that still have traces of meat, parts that have not been used. The fighting dogs drag them off to the shade. Everyone is happy when it finally ends. Mom-mah concerns herself with the details of the last event, the "wica wota," or "feasting," a banquet that occurs after the funeral, and most of the meat is put aside for this meal. About a third of the meat goes into large cooking pots to feed people throughout the wake. Some of the meat is cut into thin slices to be dried. Mom-mah calls it "papasaka." It is pounded and mixed with marrow from the bone to make "wasna," and some of the pa pa is used to make a soup. The wasna is used for the "wanġi woyute," or "spirit food" for the departed soul, food for its journey home.

I remember Keg-le's funeral as an event where everything centered around the food, its preparation, and its consumption. I also remember the feeling that it would be a festive event if only my Keg-le could be there to see what was being done and hear what was being said on her behalf. I sometimes expected her to show up next to Mom-mah or me, but she didn't. She couldn't. What was left of her lay in the center of the room in a casket surrounded by plastic wreaths, flowers, and star-patterned quilts. Star quilts and other bright geometric-patterned quilts are draped over the coffin and over the tables and benches that hold the flowers. Next to the flowers are bowls of candy and cigarettes, which are given during the wake to those who stay up all night with the body. The cigarettes and hard candies, like the slaughtered cow, are provided for those who come to participate in the wake and funeral.

Mom-mah makes sure that every detail is taken care of; everyone turns to her for direction, for advice on where to put the items people have brought, including the wreaths, flowers, and food. A close relative is constantly whispering in her ear about who brought what for the "wihpeya" or "give-away-things." The wihpeya takes place after the burial and feast. Things of value are given away to the people. This ritual is done, as all things are done, in a great circle. All the items to be given away are spread in a wide circle for all to see. When we Lakota were first put on the reservation, they arrested our people when they had a wiḣpeya for a dead relative. The ritual was against the law, they said. After we modified it and invited ministers from the Christian churches, we were once again allowed to have wiḣpeyas at our funerals.

A trunk was given to the minister who said the burial prayers. A beautiful quilt was given to the grandmother who sat diligently by the body for the entire wake. A star quilt was given to the man who made all the announcements during the wake and funeral. A five-yard piece of material and a blanket were given to the woman who did most of the cooking. A box filled with small odds and ends like bath towels, dish towels, and aprons was passed out to the people sitting in the circle, those who had come to the burial service. These things were done according to Mom-mah's wishes. No one was forgotten. The more that was given away, the more honored the dead person was. Even the food that was left over was given away, whole cakes and pies, to families who came to the funeral. They carried the food home as "wataʿca" or "leftovers from a feast." The more generous one was, the better it was in the long run for the surviving family.

Mom-mah is a generous person. I have learned to be like her, but she disapproves of me and tells me in a half-scolding way, "Kaġi śni śni ya ską." I was generous in a haphazard way, "without regard for anything." I know that Keg-le, whose naġi hovered over us those few days of the wake and funeral, was pleased when she saw Mom-mah and everything she tried to do to honor her with her overwhelming generosity to those who came.

Finally, when all the soup, frybread, cakes, pies, crackers, and "wożapi," "a boiled berry pudding," and pots of hot sugared tea and coffee were all consumed or given away; when the last bath towel was handed to the last person; when all the people began to gather their items, including their own dishes and silverware which they brought with them, the reality of Keg-le's death seemed to hit my mother. It was then, as the last person shook her hand and loaded food and give-away items into their car and left, that Mom-mah began to turn inward. Quietly she sat in her black dress, black scarf, and black sweater, fatigue showing on her face. With her head bowed down and her hands clasped in her lap, she began to openly weep. "Hąu, hąu, hąu," she cried. I stood beside her, trying to rub her back the way I remember she rubbed mine. "Cuwi wapatitą la," she would say whenever I was sick—"I rubbed her back to make her feel better." As I rubbed, her sweater awkwardly moved up and down on her hunched-over back. Underneath my hand I felt the rough sweater, and the cotton dress underneath the sweater. I kept rubbing as I tried to keep back that cold feeling in my lower body—that feeling, that flash of ice and intense heat that comes with sudden fear or realization.

Our Resurrected Selves

I remember the Easter I wore a lavender dress with white leather shoes and anklets. I remember hiding my thin, dark, knobby knees with the hem of the dress. It was the Easter my mother told me I would be baptized in the Niobrara River. The Niobrara flows into Nebraska from Wyoming to the west and out of Nebraska to the east, into the Missouri River. It is a small river, which we call "Na-huya Hohpi Wakpala," and we drove to it on hot summer days to swim. My mother had invited ministers from the Christian church, which she had joined a few years before, at the time she quit drinking.

My mother had been an alcoholic for several years. Then one Sunday, my oldest sister Keg-le invited her to a church service where the born-again Christians were praying. Mom-mah went to the service where she fell upon her knees, and when they prayed for her, she began speaking in tongues. She spoke in a tongue that she didn't know, but when the minister held the microphone up to her lips, the people praying heard her say, "For God so loved the world that he gave his only Son, that whoever believes in him should not perish but have eternal life. So saith the Lord. So saith the Lord. So saith the Lord." She kept repeating the last phrase until she fell exhausted upon the ground. Then the minister helped her to her seat. When she arose, she said she did not want to drink alcohol ever again. That feeling stayed with her as she found herself turning to the Christian church, where she was saved.

It was said that when she fell upon her knees, the Holy Spirit had alighted upon her soul, and she uttered words from the Bible that she didn't even know. She had not accepted Christianity as it was taught at the Catholic boarding school. She was only there for a short time, right before her parents left the reservation to follow the crops from town to town. She only knew and trusted the religion that her father and mother followed, but when she lost her mother in a peyote ceremony held by the Native American Church, she had lost all faith. Mom-mah said my grandmother had suffered from diabetes and was in a coma, but the people in the ceremony did not know that. She died the next morning. Mom-mah had no religion when she turned to alcohol to take away the pain.

In the years that followed her miraculous recovery from alcoholism, we were all immersed in Christianity. My older brother was the only one spared, because he was already in the Catholic boarding school. My younger brother and I, however, and my older sisters were all baptized by the ministers of the church. The two men who baptized me were elders of the church. They gently led me into the cold April thaw of the Niobrara River. I remember the riverbank where Mom-mah and others stood. The children almost ran into the water as they crowded around to see. A group of tall Lakota men stood where they had gathered a group of us who were to be baptized that day.

When it was my turn to be baptized, I walked forward, my legs wading heavily through the water in my Easter dress. I felt the current around me, the men holding me by the elbows on each side. They said, "Little sister, we now baptize you in the name of our Lord," and they dipped me backward into the cold water. My hair instantly matted on my forehead, and my dress looked "šapa," or "dirty," as I waded wet and heavy out of the water. The men then laid their hands upon my small head and prayed over me. The words I kept hearing were "Jesus, Jesus, Jesus, Jesus." On the banks of the river, I heard Mom-mah and the others say over and over, "Praise the Lord."

We left the Niobrara River and returned to the church, which was actually someone's living room. We had no church building where the services were held. They were held wherever people opened up their homes for us to come and pray. I remember driving for miles to revivals held at people's homes. Sometimes we brought a tent and camped there; sometimes we slept in the car. After my baptismal I was taken to a service where I was prayed over. The prayers were to invite the Holy Spirit to alight upon me, giving me the gift of speaking in tongues, or the ability to dance in the spirit.

During the service, I was placed in a chair in the center of the room. I was to be prayed over by the men of the church. A few women also placed their warm hands upon my head. Calling me "little sister," they prayed loudly with great fervor. They called out "Jesus, Jesus, Jesus." I sat in the middle of the circle in a small rickety chair, my feet firmly planted on the creaking wood floor. I was told to say "glory, glory, glory" repeatedly until the Holy Spirit entered into me and I was able to speak in tongues. I repeated the word over and over until my tongue tripped over it, but I could not speak in tongues. Someone held the microphone to my lips, but all that the praying people heard was a small and tired voice distinctly saying, "glo-ree, glo-ree, glo-ree."

I was disappointed and mystified. Why couldn't I speak in tongues like Mom-mah? I now know why I could not speak in tongues. I know that I was aware of it at the time, but there was nothing I could do about it: I was thinking too much. I thought about the way the praying hands pressed upon me, the way they said the word "Jesus" with such conviction, and the way I felt like a small sponge soaking it all in but unable to stand firm. I was not letting go and allowing things to happen. I thought about what the Holy Spirit might look like, and I remember feeling self-conscious and expectant at the same time. I was ready, but I was not cooperating. I never have cooperated in life. I wanted to know exactly what was supposed to happen when He alighted upon me.

I did not learn to speak in tongues, and I could not dance in the spirit as Mom-mah and others did. Wherever the service was held, the living room was cleared of all furniture. They lined the walls with benches where everyone sat. In a selected spot stood an amplifier, a microphone, and an electric guitar that was used the way an organ is used in other churches. There was no set service, but there were set aspects of the service which were predictable. There was a period when everyone gave a testimonial about the good things that had happened to them since the last church service. There was also a time in the service when those who needed prayers kneeled down and the minister came and laid his hands upon them and prayed. And then there were the times that they cast out demons from those who wanted to be cleansed. I saw them cast out a demon from a woman who spoke in a garbled voice. As she spoke, they held the microphone to her lips. When she finally vomited, the demon left her and she was herself again. I remember the demon in the woman seemed to succumb to the words "Jesus, Jesus, Jesus."

They cleared the room of all furniture, because during the service when the singing began, sometimes the people in a trance began to dance. They were taken by the Holy Spirit, and they danced. I liked the music. I remember never seeing a songbook or copies of the words to the songs they sang, but everyone seemed to know the words and music. The houses where the services were held shook with music and dance. The only song to which I learned the words was the one where everyone sang, "I saw the light, I saw the light, no more darkness, no more sorrow. Praise the Lord, I saw the light."

Once when I was very sick, my father said that he would take me to see Oral Roberts. He said that Oral Roberts was more powerful than any minister and that when Oral Roberts laid his hands upon me, I would be healed. I remember the healing services and the way the men gently put their warm hands upon me. They anointed their hands with a healing oil which came from a small bottle labeled "olive oil." Even now its smell reminds me of those hands and that time in my life.

I recall that one of the ministers in our church who was a policeman came to our car while on duty because Mom-mah had told him I was sick. In full uniform, he bent over me as I lay in the back seat, and he laid his warm hands upon me and prayed. I don't remember why I was sick. I only remember Mom-mah's testimonial that I did not have to go away to a hospital where they were to monitor a spot on my lung that had shown up in an X ray at the government hospital. Mom-mah told the people at the church service that the spot miraculously disappeared and that I had begun to feel better.

There were other parts of the service that I also remember well: for one, the way Mom-mah diligently washed her feet before the church service because she knew that the minister and others would practice the ritual of washing one another's feet. I remember all the revivals and the day that a real church was finally built. It seemed that as soon as it was built, everything fell apart.

In a faraway place, my mother said, "heci okicize"—"there was a war." It was a place that seemed very far away to us on the reservation. It was as far away as Europe, across the sea, where we lost relatives who fought in World War II. We lost relatives to the war in Korea, too, and still others died in the war in Vietnam. The war in Vietnam came and took the oldest son of our strongest minister, on whose land we had built our first and only church. The minister loved to sing and play the guitar. His son, too, played the guitar and had a band that had almost made it to Dick Clark's show, they said. He played very well. But he was drafted and went away to Vietnam. He came home in a casket sealed by the government. It was the first sealed coffin I had ever seen. A picture of him in his dress uniform was propped up on the coffin. His handsome young smiling face seemed out of place on that coffin, which should have been open for us to bid him good-bye.

The fact that it was closed seemed to make his death unreal. Maybe it was better that way. My uncle, Mom-mah's brother, came home from World War II, that is, his body came home, but his spirit did not. Mom-mah remembered that the person that had come home was not the "tiblo" or "older brother" she had known. They said he was "shell-shocked" and that he spent the rest of his life in silence. Still, it was honorable to serve in the military. There was no greater honor than to serve your people and your country, no matter what. That was what we Lakota believed. Years later, I remember how I felt when I stood in uniform, ready to serve my country. Those beliefs were strong and even pulled at me—I, who was afraid of things that were not there, did not believe in things that others did, and could not speak in tongues.

The last morning, taps were played and the minister's son was buried. Along with his son, our strongest minister buried his faith. The son who had died was his father's favorite, everyone said. I remember that morning well. It was still dark when I heard the bugler play for that boy. I was sleeping in the back seat of the car, and Mom-mah was sitting inside at the wake, keeping watch over the casket with the others. I woke up and looked out the back window of the car but saw no one. I heard only the sound of the bugle, and I felt afraid. I covered myself with Mom-mah's blanket and fell asleep again. It was the last service I remember there at that church. The army mailed the father a large insurance check to replace the life of the son he had lost, and he took the money and drank away his sorrow. His wife joined him, and our church fell apart. It was as if none of us could bear to see him reduced to the lost soul he had become.

My mother, who had spoken in tongues and danced in the spirit, put away her testimonials and seemed lost herself until the resurrection of our old religion. A new federal law was passed around the time of Nixon's resignation. We were at last allowed to practice the old religion openly. Mom-mah, with the same fervor she had had in practicing the Christian rituals, joined the new movement that revived the old rituals, as if a Jewish man named Christ had not saved her from herself the day she kneeled down before the ministers of the church and repented.

I was perplexed. How could she let it go so easily, I wondered. The Holy Spirit alighted upon her and gave her the gifts to speak in tongues and to dance blissfully in the spirit. How could she turn away from it so easily? If I had received the gifts that she had, I think I would not have turned away as she had done. Even as young as I was, I understood the mystery and the power of belief. I learned to pray in Mom-mah's church. It helped me to understand the teachings the Jesuits later tried to teach me, in high school, when I followed in my older brother's footsteps and graduated from the same Catholic high school from which he had graduated. I did not tell the Jesuits, who had me read the Gospel of Saint Mark, about the miracles I had seen. Neither did I tell them about the faith Mom-mah and the others had had in their now abandoned church; about the demons that they had cast out; nor about the Holy Spirit who had alighted upon us all, making some of us speak in tongues and dance in the spirit, and leaving others of us perplexed but open to the Word. I did not tell them that I was baptized in the Niobrara River and that I was healed. I did not tell them that they did not need to convince me. I had seen their Truth. I had lived it for awhile.

What I remember most about Mom-mah's church and how it affected my life was that they, the church, gave my mother back to me. They took her as she was and restored her. The time before she gave up her drinking I have blocked out of my memory. What I remember most was when she came out of the fog that her drinking had put her in and offered us tidbits from her pockets. These were the times that my younger brother and I were happiest. She liked raisin bread and carried it in her deep, wide pockets. I remember those days as the time when we ate raisin bread.

We had no other choice but to be her children until she herself chose to be our mother, our Mom-mah. When she came to, we forgave her for all the times she wasn't there, as Mom-mah's church taught us, "seventy times seven." That was how many times we forgave her, as many times as any young child forgives. The time after she gave up her drinking I remember well. It is a period I embrace. Her resurrection was my own.

Carnival at the Sun Dance

In mid-August, the month we call "Wasut'ų Wi," or "the month the chokecherries turn black or ripen," we would pack our old white canvas tent, tent poles, and bedding, cooking pots, and utensils, an old fire grate, two blackened coffeepots, an ax, kindling, firewood, a water bucket, wash basin, and a kerosene lamp into the back of our old car and drive forty miles to the annual Sun Dance held on the reservation. We would pack laundry baskets and old suitcases with clothes, along with dishes and eating utensils, and go. "Iglaka," Mom-mah would say, meaning "taking everything to camp or to move."

We arrived on a Wednesday night and stayed until the following Monday, when we would pack our dirty laundry, tent, and everything we had brought and drive home in the late morning. When we first got there, I would grow excited at the prospect of running free through the camp between the Sun Dance grounds, the carnival, and the rodeo. All three events were held concurrently in the center of the large camp. How difficult it was for me to decide, as a child, which event was more important.

I remember looking out the car window as we had approached the camp, at what seemed to me hundreds and hundreds of white canvas tents and tipis all along the hillside. We camped in the same spot every year, over on the east side. In the old days, we knew exactly where we should camp. It was said that we Lakota came together "waniyetu wązi cąyą," meaning "after one winter has passed." We came together not in August but in the springtime, and we camped in a great circle like the one we were making at this Sun Dance, but in a more formal and organized manner. Where each family camped would have been determined by a camp leader or leaders, depending upon the size of the camp. Back then, where we camped was determined by what band and status our family enjoyed. If we had still lived according to the old ways, I don't know where we would have camped. I belong to two bands, the Oglala and the Brulé. It is my father's mother who is Brulé. A part of me is Brulé, that part that shares the blood of my great-great-grandfather Heȟaka Išnala, a Brulé chief named Lone Elk. His daughter Nation was my great-grandmother. His grand-daughter Maza Wagmuha wį, or Iron Rattle Woman, is my grand-mother. His great-grandson is my father.

The only thing I remember about the Brulé side of my family is the long car ride, traveling north from Nebraska into South Dakota, to the Rosebud Reservation to see my aunt, who is my father's sister. She and my father considered themselves Brulé and not Oglala. It was their father, my grandfather, who was Oglala, but my father and his sisters chose to remain there among the Brulé because Brulé was what their mother was. It was the way we lived. If we were from different bands like I am, our mothers determined which side we chose. When my Oglala grandfather died, he returned to his own band. He had lived all of his adult life among the Brulé, but when he died, he went home. He is buried in an old Episcopal cemetery in Pine Ridge, along with his other relatives. My grandfather grew up there, in an area north of Pine Ridge where all of his relatives lived, in a place called Slim Buttes.

I have to reconcile these different aspects of myself, the Oglala and the Brulé sides of my "tiošpaye," "my clans." When I think about where I come from, I am reminded of the vast area of land my grandfathers, great-grandfathers, and great-great-grandfathers roamed, and the place where they considered their home to be: their sacred land, the "Ȟe Sapa," the Black Hills. I think about how free they were, about the places where they held their ceremonies and their Sun Dances, their summer camps on the plains, and their winter camps in the Black Hills.

When I was growing up, I identified with the Oglala side of my family, but I preferred my Brulé relatives, who had kind hearts like my father. Maybe it was because I did not see my cousins from Rosebud very often, so they seemed kinder; but I always looked forward to seeing them. I liked going to visit them on the Rosebud Reservation. I remember traveling with my father by car to see his sister, one of my favorite aunts. There were many small towns between the Nebraska border and the reservation, and inevitably we stopped at every one. My favorite stop along the way was a town where they had a filling station with a candy store in it. It had a large display window inside, lined with penny candy, bubble gum, and candy bars. It had racks of potato chips and jars of dill pickles and pickled pigs feet. It had oiled wood floors and a wood stove off to the side. I liked that stop because it was there that my father would buy me a bottle of orange pop and penny candy. When we arrived at Rosebud and visited my aunt, I remember how eager I was to start back on the highway again so that we could stop at that filling station. I met many of my father's relatives there at what we called Sicaġu, or "burned thigh." Their beautiful names are what I will always remember and keep with me when I think about the Brulé side of myself. They had names like Maĥpiya Ska Wį, or White Cloud Woman, and Maza Wagmuha Wį, meaning "Iron Rattle Woman."

The annual camp that I remember is what we called the Sun Dance when I was a child, and it was hosted by us Oglala. It was the only camp held among all the different bands. All of our traditional gatherings and religious ceremonies had been banned, all except for this one. People came from all the different reservations and from different states. They came from the cities, too. "T'e hataya," Mom-mah would say, "from far away." When we arrived we began asking others if "so and so" had arrived and where they were camped.

We selected a site and settled in near the eastern edge of the camp, along a fence separating the Sun Dance grounds from a rancher's grazing range for his cattle. The rancher's barbed-wire fence provided a handy clothesline for Mom-mah, and we camped right near it with our door facing the east, as always. Other relatives camped near us and stopped by to visit. Mom-mah always had coffee or tea brewing on the blackened grates over the open fire, and she always offered both coffee and tea to those who stopped by. She only drank tea, but she taught us always to offer tea or coffee to visitors, and if possible a chair or a place to sit. I learned these things and as a young child I would gladly hunt for chairs for my elders, offering tea or coffee from Mom-mah's blackened pots.

We knew exactly where our tent was among the seemingly endless rows of tents along the hillside. We parked our old car on the side of the dirt road, which wound its way through the camp. It provided privacy from the traffic passing by. Several times a day a water truck passed through, spraying the dirt road so that the fine white dust that covered everything would be less severe. At ten o'clock at night, when the dancing ended, I found my way back to the tent, unrolled my bedding, and lay down on the hard ground that was covered only by the canvas floor of the tent. I remember falling into a deep sleep only to be awakened, it seemed a short time later, by the ever-present announcer. He cleared his throat and sometimes sang a song in Lakota. At other times he would call out, "Kikta po, Kikta po," the way they said the meadowlark sings in the morning. It means "wake up, wake up." Mom-mah would join the announcer and call out "wana kikta pe," meaning "it is now time to wake up."

In those years, the campground was the thing I remembered most about the annual Sun Dance. I remember the smell of flattened sage around our camping spot, the smell of "wigliŋ kaġapi," or "bread fried in oil," and the smell of an outdoor fire in my clothes and hair. When I woke up in the morning, Mom-mah would say, "iglużaża na glasto ye," meaning "wash your face and comb your hair." She did not like any of us to appear unkempt.

"Gą s'e nażį śni ye," she would say. "Don't stand there with your hair uncombed and uncared for." To appease her, I would wash my face and comb my hair the minute I awakened. I dipped the small metal dipper into the bucket of water Mom-mah kept in the shade by the tent and filled the water basin. Using the bar of soap near the towel that hung from the tent rope, I would wash quickly in the cold water. Once I finished, I was always careful to pour the water out and lay the basin near the towel for the next person. Sometimes I washed my hair in the small wash basin, using shampoo and rinsing with cold water. We all carried our water in buckets from the hand pumps in the center of the Sun Dance grounds. I did not know back then that because the Sun Dancers danced for those four days, I was not supposed to use water like that. I was supposed to use it sparingly, and when I did use it, I was to pray for the dancers in the circle who were dancing without food or water.

The tribal government provided water, sometimes firewood, outhouses, and a daily meal of soup, bread, coffee, tea, and sometimes "wożapi," a "sweet puddinglike dessert." They policed the campground, and since alcohol was forbidden on the reservation, they jailed overnight anyone who had had too much to drink. They charged admission to the Sun Dance, and they housed the Sun Dancers and made sure that they were isolated from the rest of us. They appointed as the Sun Dance leader a man who wore a long dark wig.

I remember him well, how he led the dancers and performed the ritual of piercing the men when it was time. I remember how tall he was, and how quiet and sure he seemed as he went about his duties. He led by the hand the first man in a long line of dancers, and all of the other dancers followed them. He led the dancers as if they were all his beloved children and he was afraid for them. They followed him faithfully, keeping their faces tilted toward the sun, their eyes looking upward. While dancing they moved from a spot facing the west to a spot facing the north. All day they moved like that, from west to north, north to east, east to south, and south to west. I can still see them, the thin men moving rhythmically to the drum. The men all wore bright colors, primarily red, skirtlike garments. They were bare-chested, and each man wore a whistle around his neck, a whistle that in the old days would have been made from the wing bones of the eagle. Even now, I can hear the drum and the sound of the whistle as they danced. I can see the color red in everything they wore, including the small strands of red cloth they used to tie together the sage crowns they wore upon their heads.

A few women danced with the men, always staying behind them. It was said that in the old days the women usually danced for someone, perhaps a brother, husband, or a male relative who was absent. The women dressed in simple cotton dresses and wrapped a "šina kaswpi," or "shawl" around their waists like the men. They danced but did not get pierced, that is, undergo, on the fourth day of the Sun Dance, an actual piercing of the surface layer of the skin on the chest. "Paȟloka pi," Mom-mah would say. "They pierced." Mom-mah was referring to the way the medicine man carefully pierces the surface layer of the skin on a man's chest and inserts a slender stick. To this stick a strong leather thong is securely tied and is then attached to the tall Sacred Tree. The man dances, attached to the Tree, until he pulls himself free.

The women did not participate in piercing. Instead, they danced and prayed. In the opening prayer of the Sun Dance, the leader implores T'ųkašila or "Grandfather," "Hoye iwakiya," meaning "a voice I am sending." And "Namaȟų yo," meaning "Hear me." He prays "Wa-ni kta ca," meaning "So that I might live," "le ecamu," meaning "I do this." I watched the leader of the Sun Dancers and the way he always looked directly out at the audience, at us, as if we were a mirage and he had to keep his wits about him. He looked out at us as much as we looked in at him.

In the old days it was said that we danced because "Wi," the "Sun," was part of "Wak'ą T'ąka," or "the Great Sacred." He was our Grandfather, "T'ųkašila." He was called "Father," or

"Ate," by the people. The sun was all these things to us, and more. We danced because we wanted to please Him, our Father. We knew that if we lived a certain way that He would be pleased with us. We knew he would be pleased if we told the truth, held ourselves upright, were fearless, and lived in a compassionate way toward our people. He would be pleased if we always remembered the helpless ones, the old and feeble, and the young and small. He would be pleased if we remembered to stand up for our land and all that was ours. He would be pleased if He knew that we were grateful, that we were humble, and that deep in our hearts we felt compassion for every living thing.

We had forgotten these things, so it seemed. Once these ceremonies were banned, we lost our center. We became trapped in time and space. We no longer conversed with our Ate, our "Father," through these ceremonies. We became afraid, and everything seemed unfamiliar. If only we had turned inward when everything in which we believed had collapsed around us. If only we had remembered that inside ourselves, where everything is the color red, that the universe we believed in exists beyond time and space, then we would not have lost our way. This was what we should have remembered, but we didn't.

Like all children, I looked around me and thought that what I saw was what was real. I had not yet learned that there is much more than what we see with our eyes. As a child I attended the Sun Dance and ran around distracted by all the events there. I was interested in everything, the rodeo, the rides at the carnival, the parade on Saturday morning, and the powwow at night. I was interested in everything except the Sun Dance itself. The area where the Sun Dance was held was fenced in, and admission was charged. This was a way of allowing the tourists to come in, pay a fee, and watch the dancers in exactly the same way they could if they wanted to sit and watch the bull and bronco riders at the rodeo. All of it went on at the same time, in great haste and general confusion. In the evenings, "wi mahel iyaye caya," that is, "when the

sun went down," there was a "wacipi" or "dance" in the Sun
Dance circle. There dancers came in their full regalia and danced
and danced.

The Sacred Tree, the tall cottonwood, stood in the center with
its bright flags in the sacred colors—red, yellow, black, and white—
hanging from it. Everything revolved around it. Tickets were
sold to the nightly powwow, the rodeo, and the carnival. Cotton
candy, snow cones, candied apples, and cold cans of soda pop were
sold by vendors. The aroma of popcorn and hamburgers was in
the air. Pop cans littered the carnival and rodeo. Even the grounds
around the area of the Sun Dance were littered with the wrappings
of food and empty cans of drinks. All the while, the Sun Dancers
danced all day without food or water. Not until I was older and
attended my first real Sun Dances did I learn that to litter a sacred
area in this way was wrong. In the old days, the place where a Sun
Dance had been held was sacred ground. Nothing else was done
there.

When I was a child, I didn't know these things. It happened
one year after the Sun Dance was over that I came to fully understand the sacredness of the event. We had returned home to our
small house in Nebraska, and one day my older brother tied a
towel around his midriff, then tied a string around his neck with a
makeshift whistle on it that imitated the eagle bone whistle he had
seen the men in the Sun Dance circle use. He raised his hands and
danced facing the sun. Mom-mah was horrified. It was the only
time that she scolded him directly. He had been playing, and
Mom-mah told him that what he was doing was not play, that it
was sacred, and that the men in that circle danced because they
had a dream. It was then that I understood the inherent sacredness
of the dance. It was then that I understood that even with the
carnival, the rodeo, and the parade, and even the Miss Sun Dance
beauty pageant, that what went on in the circle mattered the most
to Mom-mah and the old ones. They knew that a man had had a
dream and was now dancing in the Sun Dance circle, praying for
his dream. They knew how hard it was to dance there in that circle

when on the third day, a Sun Dancer's mouth could become so dry that it might feel like someone had filled it with cotton. The Sun Dancer's hands might ache as if with arthritis because he was so dehydrated. I remember those feelings, when years later I danced in the Sun Dance circle as a participant and found myself thinking about how easy they had made it look—back then when I was a child and had watched them dance while I sipped a snow cone.

When the old rituals were restored to us and I was able to participate in the Sun Dance, it was not so easy for me. I remember that the need to cry filled my heart the first time I danced in the Sun Dance circle. Those first real tears ran down my face and spilled into my soul. Out there in that great circle, I realized how truly humble I was in all the universe. I felt very sorry for all the times I did not know, the times I took for granted everything that T'ukašila had given me, the times that I had accepted things without ever thanking Him. How arrogant and ignorant I had been, and still am. They knew, Mom-mah and Kah-kah, exactly what all of it meant. They kept quiet and went to the circle and watched the man in the long dark wig lead the Sun Dancers, and they prayed with him anyway. They prayed even when all of us who had paid to see it watched it like an audience at a sideshow. Mom-mah and Kah-kah prayed while the carnival rides stopped and started as people purchased tickets for a quarter; the dust at the rodeo flew as the riders with numbers pinned on their backs, dressed in their cowboy boots and brand new jeans, mounted and dismounted with each passing event. The vendors counted change and sold hamburgers, and the dancers danced. The dancers danced in the full sunlight, raising their arms to the sky, sage crowns upon their heads, sage bracelets upon their wrists and ankles. Some carried a hoop made of sage, others a fan made of sage. They danced, ignoring us as we children ran from one event to the next, spending quarters as fast as we could get them. I was like everyone else there: I ate the snow cones and cotton candy. I drank soda pop and ran around the sacred circle. I chased boys and ran to and from the carnival looking for quarters on the ground. I played and played, never once stopping, until the last day, to see the faces of the Sun Dancers. "Wicapaĥloka pi," Mom-mah had said. "They pierced." I only went on the last day because that was when the piercing was done by the man in the long dark wig. I was no different from the tourists. I wanted to see what everyone else had paid to see.

Wide Open Space

I grew up in a place where the sky overhead was my cap, and my arms and legs were extensions of the plains that stretched from where I stood to infinity. I grew up thinking the world was open and expansive. I felt satisfied in that open sky, just like at night when I look up and see and feel the silence of the stars in that wide open blackness. Years later, when I had lived on the East Coast, I periodically had to go to the shore near where I lived and see the flatness of the ocean before I felt at peace again, for a while. It was my fix, my need for that unhindered feeling of growing up and being in a place where wide open space stretches out far into the horizon. For that reason I needed to see the ocean, the clean line of the water against the sky. How it reminded me of the gently rolling hills around my home on the reservation in South Dakota. There the hills, too, touch the sky along a clear line.

There, at home in South Dakota, I know why my ancestors called the world and life a sacred hoop, a great circle. "Hoco-kat'uya," they said, or "kaowįh," that "everything was a circle" and "all things were done in a circle." When I stand outside the door of my house there, I see the horizon to the north, the east, the south, and the west surrounding me. There, where there are no other houses or buildings, I see the circle. I see myself standing in the center, just as they had millennia before me.

My early life was spent among the cornfields in Nebraska. My brother, who grew up among the children of the farmers of those

fields, hated corn. He spent his years in school feeling claustro-
phobic, determined to find the wide open space up north where
our reservation was. By the time he was in seventh grade, he had
left, never to return. He moved to the reservation to live with a
relative and to attend the government school as a day student. He
later transferred to the Catholic boarding school on the reservation because of the fighting at the government school.

My brother never escaped the feeling of claustrophobia he had
developed from the time he went into a cornfield to steal corn for
my grandfather who was hungry. He lost his way in the rows and
rows of corn. He walked for miles with only the sun above him,
going from row to row, hearing only the dizzying sound of the
grasshoppers, never sure of his directions, and convinced that he
would never get out. He grew hungry, and as the sun rose straight
above him, he said all he had to eat was the raw corn he found.
After that day he never ate corn unless it was cooked, creamed,
and came from a can.

The autumn after Keg-le, my older sister, died, we left Nebraska. Mom-mah bought a condemned house from a farmer and
had it moved thirty miles north to the reservation. The kitchen,
back bedroom, and bathroom had been left behind, and only two
bedrooms, a living room, and dining room made the long trip
north, creaking along the two-lane highway to an alfalfa field.
The farmer who owned the house plunked it down on the edge of
a small cliff and left it. Its dining room was exposed to the dry
north wind. A contractor Mom-mah hired came and tacked on
an addition with plywood floors and no insulation. This room
became Mom-mah's bedroom, where we slept those winters in
South Dakota.

A few days before school began that September, our family
made the usual pilgrimage to the reservation, this time to stay.
Mom-mah packed our car with pots, pans, dishes, clothes, and
groceries—the essentials. We followed two pick-up trucks carrying
beds, dressers, chairs, tables, stoves, cats, dogs, and a refrigerator.
The caravan of trucks and our car looked minuscule on the flat

prairie, three dots moving northward along the Nebraska plain, past the sand hills into South Dakota, where we were swallowed up by the dry rolling hills.

Once on the reservation, my older brother took it upon himself to look out for my younger brother, my grandfather, my mother, and me. We were a family, the five of us. Our two older sisters had left the reservation and moved to Chicago, which seemed a world away. They left the reservation as part of a relocation program in which they were given training in a trade school. When one of my sisters was able to take shorthand and type, she was given a job. My other sister babysat for her. They were close. I was a stranger to them but not to my brothers. My brothers were both my alter egos. The older one was intelligent, astute, and wanted to please my mother and grandfather. The younger brother was imaginative, playful, and often tongue-tied around the adults. I do not remember my sisters as well as I remember my brothers. I only remember Keg-le, my oldest sister who had been my surrogate mother before we left Nebraska for good. When she died, Mom-mah could not bring herself to live there, where memories of Keg-le were all around us in that small town; so we left and made our home on the reservation near where Kah-kah and Mom-mah had grown up.

When we first moved to the reservation, I remember the day my older brother brought home a duck that he had shot with a BB gun. He gave it to my grandfather, Kah-kah, just like he had the dozen ears of corn he had brought home for him, husked and neatly wrapped in his belt like schoolbooks, the day he was lost in the cornfield. He brought the duck home and Kah-kah cooked it. Kah-kah told him how he would have cooked it in the old way. He would have dug a hole in the ground and buried the duck with hot coals from a fire. He would have left it buried until it roasted into a delicious meal.

"Ehąnihci," my grandfather would begin, "A very long time ago," whenever he wanted to tell us something about the past, about our culture that seemed distant and indeed far in the past.

When I was younger and lived in Nebraska, I did not realize that the world I lived in was just a shadow behind a real world—a world where Lakota was spoken and the old ways were preserved in the way we addressed one another and the way we looked at one another, and even in the way we were taught to think. I no longer think in Lakota the way Kah-kah, Mom-mah, and my brothers thought. I don't know when I stopped thinking in Lakota, but I do know that when I first began to think in English, it was only on a whim. Now I am stuck with them—these thoughts which have no root in me—and somehow I have to recapture the thoughts I thought with my ancestors, the thoughts that lie buried deep in my subconscious like old roots from a great tree but a tree that is no longer alive. "Wacį ma napa," it is said in Lakota. "My thoughts are split in two." I hesitate and am often undecided as to what I should do or not do.

The duck my brother brought home reminded Kah-kah of a story, "ohųkak'ą," about Iktomi and the ducks. My brother always brought home things for us, sometimes out of necessity and sometimes out of a natural tendency to be generous, like all Lakota children. He gave and gave and gave, even to his death. The last thing I took from him because he offered it to me was a sprig of wild mint. I remember standing near him. He avoided my eyes directly, the way he wanted me to avoid his eyes directly. He wanted us to live in the old way, the way Kah-kah had lived. My brother, in his wisdom, wanted to preserve what was good in our lives.

In the old way, when the circle of the sacred hoop was whole, it was said that all things were done in a certain way. Somehow that way honored life as it was lived by the "ikce wicasa," or "the common man" as we called ourselves. My brother said that when we were older, I should not speak directly to him, out of respect for him, an older brother. He said that even when we spoke, we should avoid direct eye contact out of respect for one another. He said that if I looked him in the eye, it could be construed as disrespectful and maybe even a challenge, that when we forgot the old ways we might lose our way, perhaps the way he had in the cornfield. I listened and obeyed. I watched him and tried to imitate him.

I learned to value what he valued—his need for independence and freedom—and to respect his courage and his willingness to experience life firsthand as when he had left to attend college in southern Colorado. These were things that seemed masculine because no one in our family had gone away alone to attend college except my brother. These were things that my older sisters—when they came home for a visit and noticed how I had grown—tried to discourage, because they thought that I, being a woman, might get hurt. They tried to take me under their counsel and teach me what they knew about life. They had lived their lives in a limited way, based on their perception of themselves as female. They felt safe in that limited role and were always looking for the perfect husband to make them complete. I, on the other hand, had been a pupil of my older brother too long and had accepted his definition of what I might be. I had no interest in anything feminine and even in the possibility that someday I might have to marry someone. I felt I had nothing to learn from my sisters, who hated the wide open space and preferred the skyline of Chicago.

When I think of our house in that wide open alfalfa field, and all around us that wide open space, I know why I prefer that place to anywhere else. I grew up there unhindered, unhurried, and always sure of where my house stood and where I belonged. It was a place where I could play without interruption or harm. It was there that I discovered that whenever I stood outside our house, I could see the horizon to the north, east, south, and west, and that if I twirled myself around, I would see the never-ending circle all around me. If I threw myself into the haystack in the alfalfa field, I could lie with my face turned up to the sky and see the circle. It was everywhere I was.

It was in that place that Kah-kah told us the story about Iktomi, the trickster who was walking one day near a riverbank when he heard ducks singing. He felt hungry and approached the flock as they sat plump and sure in the water and sang out to one another. Iktomi was always hungry. He was sure he could trick the ducks and in his usual tricksterlike way find a good meal. He approached the ducks and said in a loud voice, "K'ola," meaning "friend," in a masculine way. He addressed them as friends and told them that he had a new dance to teach them. The ducks, who were always ready to learn a new dance, responded by imploring Iktomi to sing for them and teach them.

Iktomi gladly instructed them and showed them how to do the new dance. He told them that as part of the new dance they should listen to the words of the song as he sang it and close their eyes when he told them to. The ducks agreed to do as he said. Iktomi then took a large stick, and using it to keep rhythm as he would if he had a drum, he began to sing. When he came to the words, "Close your eyes, close your eyes and dance," the ducks did so, and as a duck passed near him, he used the large stick to club it over the head. In this way, Iktomi hoped to get all the ducks so that he could enjoy a great feast. A few minutes passed as Iktomi sang the words, "Close your eyes, close your eyes and dance," and one duck, growing suspicious, opened his eyes in time to see one of his companions fall dead to the ground. The duck called out in alarm, and his flock flew away before Iktomi had the opportunity to use the stick again.

Kah-kah said that Iktomi, satisfied that he had enough ducks for his feast, prepared a fire. He dug a hole and waited for the coals in the fire to heat so that he could use them to roast the ducks. When the coals were ready, he lined the hole with them and buried the ducks he had prepared for roasting. He sat back to enjoy his success. He leaned against a tall tree, and just as the first smells of the roasting ducks reached him, he heard a loud creaking noise above him. Iktomi looked up to see two high branches above him rubbing against each other. "Hecṵp śni yo," he said. "Don't do that." The branches continued to sway in the wind and to rub loudly against each other. Iktomi became annoyed with them. "You are brothers," he said, "and you must not fight." The branches stopped for a while, but as soon as Tʻate began to blow, the noises the branches made started up again. "Wanahup śni," Iktomi said. "They choose not to listen."

Iktomi decided to intervene on behalf of reason, which he knew nothing of, and he slowly climbed the tree to try to pry the two branches apart. When he reached the high branches, he was able to pry them apart just as a strong wind blew across the prairie. His arm became wedged between the two branches. He pulled and pulled until he felt weak and could no longer pull without cutting himself. He sat in the tree, unable to move; below him he spotted a "śukmanitu," a "coyote" approaching with his nose to the ground, sniffing and looking around as if he was closing in on something. "Kaki ya a ḣo iyayayo," Iktomi called out. "Go away." The śukmanitu looked up to see Iktomi sitting in an uncomfortable position with his arm stuck between two large branches. "You cannot have the roast duck I have buried near where that stick sits under that tree," he said, pointing to where he buried the ducks. "Hena mitʻawa," he said. "They are mine." The śukmanitu became curious and sat down to watch Iktomi, who became even more angry.

At this point in the story, Kah-kah would say, "Eśa inila yȧke śni," or "He should have stayed quiet." The śukmanitu, who like Iktomi was always hungry, walked to the spot that Iktomi had told him about and began digging with his paws. Soon the delicious smell of roast duck reached Iktomi, who sat hungry and helpless in the tree while the śukmanitu enjoyed the feast that was to be his. He finished everything but the bones. Meanwhile, another big wind blew across the plains and freed Iktomi from the tree. He climbed down in time to see the śukmanitu lumber away, full and satisfied. Kah-kah, whose story was finished for now, would then say to us, "Śkatapo," meaning, "Go play." He promised to continue the story another time, for Iktomi had other adventures, enough for many stories.

Kah-kah sat in an old favorite chair by the front porch of the house, where I first became aware of the land around me and how

I was connected to it. His favorite chair was from an old ice cream parlor, and it had a twisted metal back that looked like a heart with circles in it. The seat was hard and of wood, and the legs of the chair were metal, and looked sturdy and strong. He would sometimes tip the chair back and lean against the peeling white paint of the house with his face turned up toward the sun. His long thin fingers and gnarled hands cupped his cane, which he used to stabilize himself as he napped. His favorite spot, to the right of the front door, did not have a blade of grass upon it, for we did not have a lawn. Our front yard extended out into ten acres of cultivated farmland.

Our front door opened onto an alfalfa field, which stretched to the south along a dirt road, about a mile from the highway. By the time you had reached the highway, a different world zoomed by, one of cars, trucks, and school buses. It was a world that did not exist as such when Kah-kah had been a little boy. He lived in a world of horse-drawn wagons and unpaved roads called wagon trails. He grew up at a time, after the massacre at Wounded Knee, when everyone accepted the reservation life, so it seemed, and whole families with all their belongings piled on the wagons went visiting or were on their way to find work somewhere far from the isolation of the reservation. Kah-kah knew the best places to camp between the reservation and the Nebraska state line. He knew the watering holes and the names of the places that were landmarks to the people who traveled along the road. He also knew where certain battles had occurred. He told us about the woman who was stolen by our enemy, the "Kągi," or "Crow tribe," how she returned safely, because she knew how to hide during the day and run at night to reach her own people. He told us about the boy who was scalped by the Kągi and lived to tell about it. He knew things about the land and the people whose land it was that he took with him and I will never hear. When I ride through the roads I remember driving with him as a small child, I try to listen as if I can hear him talking in that old way as he points here and there.

Kah-kah sat looking toward the road, perhaps thinking about the trips he had made by wagon, the people he had known who had since traveled down the spirit road, the "waṅǵi cąku," and about his own mother who they said had the power of a medicine woman in her old age. They said his mother's name was Keglezela Wį, or Spotted Turtle Woman, just like my oldest sister who had died. She had her own medicine, and it was said that people came to her for healing.

Keglezela Wį, my great grandmother, must have known how to use roots and herbs to make medicine in the old way, how to take the flower named "cone flower" in English, the one we call "napeośtą," which means "to put on your hand," and then to boil the root for medicine. She must have known how to take white prairie clover, the one we call "t'okala peźuta," meaning "fox-medicine," and use it to heal. She may have known how to use bittersweet, that plant that we call "woȟlokapi śni peźuta"; and perhaps how to use the root of the "hu pestola," the "common yucca plant" that grew along the hillside and was used for soap for hair, to kill lice, and to make one's hair grow long and thick. She must have known how to boil sage or wild mint for a tea to soothe a stomachache. Kah-kah's mother would have known how to do these things to help the women who came to her for medicine.

Many of these things are forgotten. The medicine men today do not know how to use herbs for medicine. It was said that long ago, when a medicine man needed a specific medicine, or "peźuta," that it would reveal itself to him as he walked along the hillside praying and searching. A specific plant would stand out more than the others, and the medicine man would use that for his peźuta. That was when God himself walked with us. The time when we were in His favor because we lived on that wide open space with grateful and glad hearts. The way Mom-mah said that all of our relatives lived in the spirit world with glad hearts.

I think about Keglezela Wį, my great-grandmother, as I grow older, and about her medicine. Mom-mah once showed me the place where Keglezela Wį is buried, a spot underneath a pine-covered ridge, a beautiful place. We buried our relatives in beautiful places where their spirits would journey from this world to the next, before they told us we had to be buried in stark cemeteries in the Christian way.

I know Kah-kah thought a lot, because he sang a lot, songs that I can still hear, that I find great comfort in, like the sound of the "táśi yagnupa," or the "meadowlark," singing in that wide open space. It was said long ago that the meadowlark would sing "Kikta po, wąna ąpa yelo," in the masculine voice. "Wake up, wake up, it is morning now." That was the way Kah-kah awoke every morning at sunrise and tended the fire in the wood stove. "Kikta po, wąna ąpa yelo," he would say. "Just like the meadowlark."

My grandfather sat looking toward the road up until the day he died in his ninety-seventh year. He watched the road for visitors, perhaps for the curious things we call "iye cįkįyąka" or "that which runs on its own," the automobile. He watched for the school bus. When it stopped, its brakes made loud noises, its red lights blinked on and off, and its door opened wide with loud squeaking sounds. Our cousins who lived off the same dusty road, my brother, and I spilled out of the bus making even louder noises. We must have been a curious sight to Kah-kah.

He was happy to see us, sometimes playfully tripping us with his cane, his "sak ye," which is pronounced "sah-ge." We ran by him on our way to watch television, or to grab something to eat. He did not call us by our English names, for he had his own names for each of us, names that he alone used. I was not fond of the name he had for me, but I understood how he could not pronounce words we took for granted in a language that was very foreign to him. My cousins and siblings did not appreciate their names either, but we knew it was Kah-kah when he called us by those names. I remember one cousin whose name was "Jerry" whom Kah-kah had renamed "Ba lo." One day after school, Jerry sat next to Kah-kah and patiently tried to teach him how to pronounce his name. He said, "Kah-kah, Jerry, emaci yab, Jerry." What he had implored was, "Jerry, Grandfather, my name is

Jerry." Kah-kah listened patiently, smiling and nodding, and finally after several unsuccessful tries, Kah-kah said, "Oh han, Jenny," meaning "I understand now what your name is in English, it is Jenny!" After that, my cousin, who played basketball, had many girlfriends, and later went to Vietnam, preferred "Ba lo" to "Jenny."

Kah-kah was a meticulous old man who wore his shirt buttoned up to the neck, the way I have seen Sitting Bull wear his shirt in pictures. He wore neat leather slippers and kept everything he owned in a large black trunk. I remember how everything about him seemed to grow thin and transparent as time went on and I became more and more aware of him growing older—his slender fingers, his thin legs, and his long feet; the long underwear he wore and the way his legs bowed when he walked. He liked to sit by the front door with his "otʿaśośe" can, an empty one-pound coffee can that he used as a "spittoon." He loved tobacco, sardines, and coffee. He sat outside, especially when the weather was warm, watching the road, the alfalfa field, and the dust flying on the road as a visitor pulled up to say hello. He was always happy to see whoever it happened to be and would call out "Ho he, ho he," words meaning, "I am pleased." I was at school the day he died. My fifth grade teacher called me to the principal's office, and Mom-mah came and took me home. I saw him lying on his bed, covered with a white cloth. They said he had died peacefully, at home.

My brothers lost a friend and a father when Kah-kah died. My older brother came home from boarding school looking shaken, like he had when he said he saw a ghost when we were smaller and younger. My younger brother searched the wood pile all day in his sorrow, unable to play, not knowing what he was looking for. I was afraid of my brothers, afraid of their collective sorrow, their feeling of loss. I watched my younger brother kick the wood chips and scatter them. I saw my younger brother's red eyes and runny nose and worried about what tomorrow might bring for all of us, now that my mother was alone.

Winter

I remember winters as cold and stark, especially the cold month of December, the month we call "Tʿahe kapśu Wi," meaning "the moon in which the deer shed their horns." We had a word for each of the months and even the phases of the moon. The words for a new moon, Witʿaca tʿe, literally translated mean "the moon died." The face on the moon, when it is a full moon, to us is a woman whom we call "Hoke Wį." "Wį" means "woman," and we say that "the woman is heavily dressed in many layers of clothing." When the moon is full, we say she has made a fire and is stirring a kettle. The old people said "wana woza yelo," or "now the woman on the moon is ladling soup out of the kettle."

We had words for all the seasons as we knew them: summer is "bloketu," autumn is "ptąyetu, winter is "waniyetu," and spring is "wetu." The worst of these is waniyetu. I remember the snow and arctic wind from the north. The wind we called the cleansing wind. It clears your head. It makes you look up at the stars in the night, look at the vastness of space. It makes you remember how insignificant you are compared to nature. It humbles you.

I remember a photograph of two children that someone had put onto canvas. An artist had painted their faces close up. The picture was of two children at Wounded Knee, the place were the U.S. Army massacred three hundred men, women, and children. Wounded Knee is a mysterious place, even today. A great sadness seems to sit quietly upon the place. It seems to embrace you when you stop there, as you are compelled to do, to see the mass grave upon the hill. "Cakpe Opi," it is called, "Wounded in the Knee," and it was there that a chief named Big Foot staked a white flag in the ground and surrendered on the night of December 28, 1890. On the morning of the twenty-ninth, for reasons too numerous to explain, the U.S. cavalry, the same Seventh Cavalry that had fought at the Battle of the Little Big Horn where Custer was killed, opened fire upon 340 men, women, and children. It was said that over 250 of them were women and children.

I saw a vision there once: I saw rain destroy the earth. The water fell like bullets upon the grass and killed all living things. In the middle of the destruction, I saw a rainbow emerge. Its brilliant colors gently touched the earth in the spot where the killing occurred. I saw the rainbow touch the earth like a medicine man gently touching the wound of a person with his fan made from the wing of an eagle. The rainbow emerged, touched the flattened grass, and faded as the sun broke through the hard-driving rain. The sun bathed everything with a yellowish light. It is said that the spirits, the "wanaǵi," love the color red, but also they love yellow, the color of the sun. Perhaps in my vision I had seen the spirits that live there at Wounded Knee. There in that place where they said a medicine man named Zįtkala Zi, Yellow Bird, had blown his eagle bone whistle to encourage the men to protect the people, the helpless ones, the old, and the women and children, when the cavalry opened fire. I have seen men, like Yellow Bird, blow the eagle bone whistle, with their faces turned toward the sun. They look up, singing, "Wanikta ca lecama yelo," which means "I will live, and that is why I do this."

What I remember most about Wounded Knee is the picture of two children, a brother and a sister standing outside a canvas tent. The year might have been 1940 or 1950. The brother and sister stood smiling in front of the tent. The girl stood without a hat, coat, or mittens. They both wore dark clothes, and the girl's hair was cropped short. They looked like Jews in pictures I have seen of the concentration camps. In the picture the girl stands next to her brother, while behind them snow covers the landscape. A stovepipe sticks out of the center of the tent. Everything in the picture is black and white, except for their bare arms, which were painted a pale blue to reflect the extreme cold. When I think of winter, that picture returns to me.

I wonder who they are, that brother and sister. Their innocent faces are not different from my own at that age. They could have been me and my older brother. Our parents lived in canvas tents like that in the middle of farm fields in Nebraska; even when they took away our buffalo hide tents, we still preferred tents.

I was born in a tent. I was born in a canvas tent in a field across from where a Jack-and-Jill grocery store now stands in that small town in Nebraska where I lived for the first ten years of my life. I was told that I was born there. I was born in late spring, right before summer, when the star we call "It'okob u" shone in the northwest, indicating that the birds have returned. "It'okob u" means "come round again," as all the seasons and natural cycles do. My ancestors knew when summer began by what stars shone in the heavens. Today we do not remember the names they gave the stars. We do not remember under which stars the seasons come and go.

I try to imagine what it was like in June of the year I was born, the month we call "Tipsila nahca Wi," or "the month the wild turnips blossom." The day I was born, my paternal grandfather came and wrapped me in soft deerskin. He brought sweets for my mother called "waskuyeca," he gave me my childhood Indian name, and he sang a song for me. He named me Badger Woman. Hoka Wį, or Badger Woman, is a name that my aunt had had, and her aunt before her. The name I was given belonged to his daughter, and through it he gave a name to my spirit. The spirit, we Lakota believe, is not born with us but is given to us at the time of our birth. So it was that at my birth he sang a song, not solely for me, but also for the spirit of all the "Badger Women" who had come before me. I was told that my grandfather came and honored me. He must have come knowing, as all Lakota know, that anything born must also die, and that death is an inseparable part of life. Perhaps he came feeling sorry for the second child born to his only son. I believed, well into my adulthood, that my grandfather and father had wished that I had been a boy when I was born. Since my father's firstborn was a girl, they might have come hoping that my father's second child would be a boy. I grew up thinking that perhaps I had disappointed them. Yet, when I heard my father call me "daughter," I knew that like any parent he accepted who I was. I grew up under the shadow of boys. I grew up believing that that would be my role and refusing in my own way to accept it.

My father's father, my grandfather, his green eyes and red bandana wrapped around his neck, was a tribal policeman. His green eyes came from his half-French father. My paternal grandfather is one-quarter French, having the blood of a trapper who came down from Canada and married a woman from the Oglala band. All we know of the trapper is that his name was Dion, and nothing more. My grandfather was proud of his French blood, his Indian blood, and his horses. Some people say that he was a horse thief, which was valued in the old days when my grandfather would have painted vividly his exploits in horse stealing upon the inner walls of my grandmother's tipi, for all to see. My father says that he had many horses and that he drove those horses from the Rosebud Reservation into the Pine Ridge Reservation, through Porcupine Creek and up past the Badlands. My father grew up on horses. I grew up afraid of them.

We called them Hema Kosiksica, or Bad Hills, and we shunned them—the place in the Badlands where my grandfather returned with his horses every year. My paternal grandfather went there remembering his father. His father, a half-French Lakota, became a "shirt-wearer" among his people. In my tribe, a "shirt-wearer," one who is said to wear "a large shirt," "ogle t'ąka ų," is a leader. They say both Red Cloud and Crazy Horse were shirt-wearers. They were "blotá hunka," meaning "leaders." My great-grandfather belonged to Red Cloud's "tiošpaye," or "extended family."

His mother, a full-blood, was from that family. She gave birth to
that side of me that is part French-Canadian. I am thankful that
my great-grandfather, my grandfather, and my father married full-
blood Lakota women, so that the French in me is less than it had
been for my great-grandfather. According to the Bureau of Indian
Affairs, my blood quantum level is one-sixteenth French. They
keep track of it so that they know just how "Indian" I am. I remember how I compared my hands to those of my full-blood Lakota cousins, how their hands seemed a richer color, especially the
folds of the skin in their knuckles as they held out a hand to me in
play. My hands in comparison seemed less sure, my fingers longer,
more slender, and my knuckles a lighter color. Perhaps it was the
French in me, hidden there in the folds of my knuckles.

My great-grandfather hid with his band of people in the Makʻo
Sica, the Badlands. It was said that he hid from the army in the
gullies of a mesa named after him. He hid in a place from where,
he believed, they could escape north to Canada, like Sitting Bull
and his people. In the winter, "waniyetu ca," that is, "sometimes
in the winter," the Badlands are covered in snow, and there is no
shelter from the wind except in the deep gullies. If you follow the
road from Porcupine, the town that is called Pȟahį Sįte, or Porcupine Tail, twenty miles north to where the Badlands begin, you
will find the first road leading west, to a high and wide plateau
with deeply eroded sides. If you follow that road, soon you'll reach
the top of the mesa. In the Badlands these mesas are called "tables." The tableland that you'll come to when you take that road
is named after my great-grandfather. The sage grows thick along
the road. At the top of the table you will see the flat land that
farmers now cultivate. The road runs straight west across the plateau. When the road cuts north, it leads straight down from the
table toward the Cheyenne River, the river we called "Sihiyela
Wakpala," which runs west into the Missouri River. Where the
tableland ends and the muddy river begins, you will see the rem-
nants of my great-grandfather's camp. It is in a place where the

winter wind whips down over the mesa, sweeping over the encampment. It is sheltered and near water.

It is a place where my great-grandfather held councils, a place where, in the darkness of night, he made many false starts north toward Canada. Today, they have built government houses there, houses that now stand ramshackle, some abandoned. After they put us on reservations, we seemed to have lost the will to live in a way that our ancestors had, in dwellings that were harmonious with the land. Our ancestors' dwellings were made of ten or twelve buffalo hides sewn together in the form of a circle, like a cape, which is draped over three strong poles with other poles leaning against the base. Such a dwelling stood fifteen to eighteen feet high. It belonged to the woman. It was called "ti," or "dwelling," "Wati," meaning "I live there," "watiki̧ hel," meaning "at the place I dwell," or "Tuwa hel ti he?" which means "Who lives there?" It is said that since the dwelling belongs to the woman, it is she who gives permission to her man, allowing him to paint his dreams or feats in battle or horse stealing on the inner walls. It is said that only a man paints realistic figures of humans and animals, while a woman paints geometric designs—squares, triangles, and lines. One is abstract, the other rooted in the here and now. One is able to dream real dreams, and the other is only able to relive nightmares. It was said that we slept in our tipis in a circle, upon buffalo robes, heads to the wall and feet toward a fire pit dug in the center of the tipi. We assigned a place in the tipi, in the circle, for each person—man, woman, and child. After the reservations came into being, we forgot all of this. It was as if we awoke in the night, in the middle of a nightmare, from which we have not yet awakened.

We no longer hold councils like they did. We no longer have leaders like my great-grandfather, who "oyate ki̧ u̧siwica ki̧ la," that is, who felt "great pity or compassion for the people." Today the winters come like they did when he was alive, but now there is no one to find the best shelter from the arctic winds. The houses the government so hastily put up cannot withstand the wind. At night, when I am there, I can hear the wind crying through the cracks in the cheap windows. It cries because we have become disconnected and disenfranchised. I know why my grandfather and father preferred to live in canvas tents. My great-grandfather would not have believed that this is the way we would end up living, without councils, without leaders, without compassion.

I remember the winters in South Dakota through the 1960s, when people lived in canvas tents. I remember some of them were my relatives. I remember visiting a distant cousin who lived with her husband and six children in a canvas tent along Porcupine Creek. Her tent looked dark from the rubber tires they burned to keep warm. Their floor was the frozen earth and a thin canvas covering. They had a small wood-burning stove, which they used for cooking and heat. Her children developed tuberculosis, and they were moved into a house that the government brought from a closed military base. That was the year they brought many of the houses we called "igloo" houses because it was said that they were brought from Alaska. They brought them and plunked them here and there on tribal land, and people moved into them. I remember walking into one and admiring the tiled floors and clean white walls. They were equipped with indoor plumbing, bathrooms, and running water. I remember some families kept their outhouses in the back, never fully trusting the indoor plumbing. It was a time when our family lived in a house that my mother bought from a farmer in Nebraska and had it moved to the reservation. I felt some solace in the fact we did not receive our house from the government. Mom-mah's house was her own, one that she bought on her own. I did not mind the fact that we still lived the old way, with a hand pump for drawing water and an outhouse equipped with a Sears catalog, because it was our house. We did not have to worry about the plumbing in a place where there were no plumbers.

I was not born in the winter, but I remember the long winters. I was conceived in September, the month we call "Cǎwap'e gi Wi"

or "the moon in which the leaves turn brown." I became aware in
my mother's womb in the middle of winter. In the old days children like me learned to live through these long winters by playing
games. One game, called "Wazi m.ni acaǧa," would have been
my favorite had I lived in those times. In this game one dipped a
branch in water and froze it by placing it outdoors, and then licked
it like a Popsicle. "Popsicle" was one of a few English words that
Kah-kah, my maternal grandfather, could say without difficulty.
He confidently used the word "pop," so that once a month on
our way into town, when we lived on the reservation, Kah-kah
would fondly say in Lakota, "When we get into town, I will buy
you pop, popcorn, and Popsicles." As a child, I loved these things,
even in winter.

I first became fully aware of my world those first winters in
South Dakota when the wind chill drops below zero and the car
battery dies. The times when Mom-mah's laundry did not dry and
she brought it into the house all frozen and left it steaming by the
wood stove. She had long clotheslines, and all the dresses, shirts,
pants, and socks stood stiff and frozen. I remember Kah-kah's
long underwear, hanging with Mom-mah's laundry. Kah-kah was
a tall man, and his long underwear stretched to the ground. I remember the times I went out to the woodpile and gathered wood
chips for the fire to try to thaw out the laundry. The cold December nights when the stars seem to take over the night sky. In the
cold dark night they seem to sparkle while everything is frozen for
a solid still moment. I often stood outside to see the stars on those
winter nights, my teeth chattering as I stood there waiting to see
how much cold I could really stand. The nights pass slowly there
in the winter. In the morning you find the sun shining weakly far
out on the eastern horizon, back over the ridge where it competes
with the clouds all winter. The role the sun plays in the winter is
neutral; all power belongs to winter. The cold is everything. It can
overpower you if you are not careful. For that reason Mom-mah
carried a blanket in the car, just in case. We lost many relatives and
friends, young and old, to the cold subzero winters. They died,

like many others, when their secondhand cars, "Indian" cars we call them, stalled along the roadside, and no one came by all night, and they fell asleep in their cold cars, never to awaken. It happened many times—sometimes alcohol was blamed—but those of us who had lived there through many winters know that it can happen to anyone. "Tasaka pi," my mother would say. "They froze to death," just like the people who were wounded at Cȧkpe Opi, or Wounded Knee. They were left to freeze in the snow.

Lakota Words

I grew up in a time before the old ways disappeared completely and the new ways emerged in their place. I think of it as a time just before sunrise when the morning dew clings to you and as the sun rises, the dew dries before your eyes. If I had had time-lapse photography, I could have watched it dry molecule by molecule, the way I now watch the old ways disappear.

I watched them disappear with my maternal grandfather. I saw Kah-kah die and take with him words that will never be used again. Kah-kah used words to depict a way of life that has forever disappeared. Our way of life was tied to our language, the way we addressed each other: brother, sister, father, mother, grandfather, grandmother, uncle, aunt, and cousin; the way in which we described our emotions, both publicly and privately; the way we described a smile, a wave, or a Lakota mannerism; the way my mother could describe a person with one word, a word that says everything and nothing, that creates an image which you both appreciate and dread. "Oh, I know people like that," you would say.

I now watch my mother—she too is battered by time—drying up like the dew right before my eyes. She too will take with her words that her father used, words that were used in the daily course of life, before English, its sterile sounds and double meanings, invaded our world and our language. In Lakota, when you say something, it can be taken literally. In English you can say something and mean the opposite, or you can be sarcastic and biting. In Lakota when you say something, it is taken as truth unless, of course, you are a liar. "Owewak'ąk'ą s'a," they would say about you. "She lies." They would never say it to you to your face. They would listen to you as if you spoke the truth, but they would know that you are a liar and would have already known that before you began to speak, and everything you say is taken in light of that truth. In Lakota everything is black or white, unpleasant or pleasant, indirect or direct, disrespectful or respectful. In English the nuances are many, and they can be overwhelming to one whose native language is not English.

I remember struggling well into my adult life with the pronunciation of certain English words. The three years I spent in a government school on the reservation prepared me for nothing more than a mediocre understanding of English. In those early years, my tongue tripped over it. I spoke it flatly and without emotion. I could not adjust my voice to its tone and pitch, and I hated it. I learned defensively to say "I don't know" as slowly and deliberately as possible. I used those three words to answer any and all questions: "I don't know." Then, one day in great irritation and frustration, my older brother lashed out at me, "Don't ever again say 'I don't know.'" He said angrily in Lakota, "Slolya yelo," meaning, "You know, I know you know." That contrary part of me, that part of me that knows that I should defer to an older brother in respect said, slowly and deliberately, in Lakota, "Slolwaye śni," which means "Know these things I do not," literally translated.

There are words in Lakota that are used to describe things in our language which have been a part of our lives since time began: words like "cąte," "ableza," and "olową," which respectively mean "heart," "perception," and "song." These are words that we say with eloquence. "Mi cąte," we say, "my heart," and "mi cąte ataya," "with my whole heart," or "mi cąte ų okihisniya," meaning "my heart is not in it." All of our emotions—happiness, joy, excitement, sadness, anger, malice, sorrow, and even love— are expressed using the word "cąte," "the heart."

It is a word that contains all that we are as a people. It expresses our longings. We say "Cạte awacɪya," meaning "My heart longs for it." Literally translated it means "My heart lacks it, therefore I long for it." Of all the words using "cạte," I prefer "cạte t'ɪza," a word that I've heard Kah-kah and Mom-mah use over and over again. It means, literally, "heart that is firm," or simply, "to have courage, to be courageous." "Cạtemat'ɪiza," they would say. "My heart is firm." They were right; they did have courage, great courage, to be able to live as they did, to lose the things they loved—their language and the old ways—and to guard what they had by retaining what they could with their hearts firm and strong.

In the same way, we are a people that say "ableza ye!" in the feminine voice, which means "try to see it, perceive it." Or we say "awableza," which means "see it clearly, be alert for it." In a similar way we say "amableza," or "you see those things in me, you perceive those things in me." The word "olowan" means song. These are the words that we say with eloquence. My grandfather and mother are eloquent in Lakota. In English my grandfather refused to speak more than he needed to. My mother accepts English as something that is necessary to know in order to get by in the world, but her language of choice, the one she enjoys, is Lakota. "Malak'ota," she would say. "I am Lakota." In English she might say "furnitures" when she meant to use the word "furniture," just as my grandfather would declare to his lessees who leased his reservation land, "You helpa me, I helpa you, and we helpa we." They did not use English unless it was necessary, and because of their rejection of English, I had to learn both.

In a conversation, my mother utters the old words effortlessly, words that I have to repeat silently to myself, my tongue and throat adjusting to the guttural, to the tone, and to the feeling that I could never speak it as smoothly as she did. I quietly jot down the old words, afraid sometimes to ask her what they mean, afraid that I would lose her confidence in me if I did ask. She believes that I know and will remember all the words I have heard spoken in her home, all the words that she and her father have used to depict a life that I will never know. I am tempted to say, "Slolwaye śni, slolwaye śni, slolwaye śni," or "I don't know, I don't know, I don't know." One day she told me, "They are bringing the language back. They are teaching it again," she said. I wait for the "but," the qualifier that one who is knowledgeable about these things always says when speaking to one who is less knowledgeable. I know my mother, and I wait for her to finish her observation. She is "ksapa" or "wise" in the old traditional sense, and she refuses to move in either direction, as acceptor or rejector of this new movement to preserve the language. "As," meaning "but," she continues, "some of the people involved in reviving the language are those who learned it from the dictionary. If you notice they say 'd' when they mean to say 'l.' They confuse the dialects," meaning the Dakota dialect with the Lakota dialect. She said that there are some who know the old language and can speak it precisely. She does not include herself among them.

I remember once she told me, "The waśicu's religion is weak. He only prays on Sunday." "Kiksuya ye," she said. "You remember that." Mom-mah said our religion is strong, and she said if you believe it, it is even stronger. "Wacekiya ye," she said. "You pray, like we pray, every day. Every moment we remember to, we pray." I remember hearing her early in the morning. "Kableza acą," as "the sun rises," after she puts on a pot of tea, she prays.

Her prayers reach far beyond time and space. She prays with her old words spoken calmly and confidently. Her words sound like the word "onomatopoeia," repeated over and over. Onomatopoeia, onomatopoeia, onomatopoeia. She prays, "T'ųkaśila, ųśųlapiye. Awąuyąkapi ye. Taku ecųk'ų pi hena ųkisakib mani ye. T'ųkaśila, mi cįca kį tuktektel ųpi kį hena awąwicakyąka ye. Ąpetu wą lecel ųkinaźį pi kį le nitawa. Mititakuye oyas'į." Her prayer translated means, "Grandfather, pity us. Look upon us with mercy. Whatever we do, walk beside us. Grandfather, my children, watch over them wherever they are. For this day in which we stand belongs to you. For all of my relatives, I pray."

I know if I looked in upon her as she prays in the quiet kitchen while her tea brews on the gas stove, her posture would be humble: her hands demurely set in her wide deep lap, her head bowed and tilted slightly. Her posture belies the nature of her prayers. She is not humble. She is the earth itself perpetuating life even as death is all around her. Even as everything breaks down and things fall apart, she stays constant.

Her prayers remain the same. Each morning before anyone else awakens, she makes sure that her gentle persistent prayers are heard. She makes sure that "T'ųkašila," "Grandfather," as He awakens the world this and every morning, is reminded of her presence. In the old language, she reminds Him that we are still here, that the language He gave to us is still spoken in gratitude. She prays always for life for others, and for pity for herself, she who sits like a mountain each day, unmovable and unchanging. I have heard that whatever you wish or pray for others, you will get. I see this truth in her. She prays for life for others, and while those she prays for each morning, each moment of every day, die, she lives.

When I hear her speak the language the way it should be spoken, I want to speak like her. I want to be like her. I want to remember the old words, the sound of my own name as it was given to me, "Hoka Wį he miye," "Badger Woman, that is who I am." I want to write down the old words, the fond way she refers to her "tiwahe," her family. She calls her brothers by their honored names: she calls a younger brother "misų"; she calls an older brother "tiblo." She is the only female in a family of five men. "Wįyą Išnala" is her Indian name. "Only Woman." That is who she is in Kah-kah's family.

I am not as confident as she is, and I do not use these words to describe my younger brother and my older brother. It is not that I have forgotten; I have not learned how to be comfortable using these words the way she does. "Ate," she calls her father. "Ina mitawa ki he," she says of her mother. She knows her relatives twice removed, "taku kiciyapi," or "the way they are related." I try to write down what she tells me. "Wicotakuye hena slolkiya

ye," she tells me. "Know who your relatives are." She considers
that knowledge important so that bloodlines are kept pure, because it was considered taboo to marry a relative, no matter how
distant. These were the things she wanted me to know.
She wanted me to know who my cousins were. I would call a
female cousin "cep'ąśi." I would call my male cousin "śiceśi."
I have heard her use these words fondly. I have heard her honor
her relatives with these names, embracing her female cousins.
"T'ożą," she calls her nieces, and "t'ośka," she says to her ne-
phews. I try to be like her, to carry around all the things that the
old way and the old language require that I remember: the things
I need to know to keep myself together, to keep myself from falling apart. I want to remain constant like her. I want to remember
to pray, to remember to sit in a humble way while deep inside my
strength is like the earth. I try to be more patient than she is—the
way she says she waits for dawn to pray, "każążą aye cąyą," meaning "as the light appears at dawn." I know that unless I write the
things I want to remember—the old words and my connection to
those around me through them—I will forget, and the sun will
rise and these things that she told me to remember, "Kiksuya ye,"
will dry up, molecule by molecule.

Wašicuia ya he?
Do you speak English?

I did not learn how to write a composition in English until I left the government school and entered seventh grade at a small school run by nuns from the Notre Dame order. I discovered that despite their shortcomings, the nuns brought people, volunteers, to the school, who were intent on teaching. There, at the school with its simple white buildings closely nestled in a small valley, I learned to read, write, and finally how to converse in English.

I learned to read properly in a program at the school, which they called a "reading lab." The lab was actually a trailer house that was equipped with small reading booths, where there were no books, only strips of film in darkened reading booths where we were required after every reading session to answer a set of comprehension questions. While there, I watched sentences flow by at a speed which I controlled and therefore could read. I could not rewind or review before answering the questions at the end of the session. I started slowly, reading at a speed that allowed me to answer the questions correctly. I enjoyed the darkened room, the quiet trailer, and the chance to learn without someone looking over my shoulder.

I remember one girl in my class who was fond of bypassing all the work. She showed me where the answers were one day when she lingered behind to point out the answer sheets in a file hidden at the end of a cabinet. I think she did it because she wanted to be my friend. We were friends all through high school. I tried to look past her shortcomings, particularly her inclination to cheat. In those early years, I seemed to have accepted people as what they were more readily than I do now. I continued painstakingly, and many times erroneously, to learn to read properly. I forced myself to try to comprehend the language I did not speak at home, the language I felt self-conscious speaking, the language I will never fully comprehend.

I learned more at that small school run by the nuns and volunteers than I learned at the government school, where I entered in the fourth grade and stayed through sixth grade. The government school, which had all the modern conveniences that the small Catholic school didn't have, seemed, by comparison, to be massive, sterile, and empty in an inexplicable way. It had desks, chairs, blackboards, and books, but it lacked something which I was not able to pinpoint until I met the nuns and teachers at the Catholic school. It had all the trappings of a school, but it did not educate the way the Catholic school did, with heart and feeling for the children in it.

The government school was worlds away from the bright classrooms I left behind in rural Nebraska. There were no sweet-smelling teachers in rouge who hung snowflakes and valentines in the windows. There was no daily reminder to "Put on your thinking cap," and no daily practice with reading or writing. There were no libraries or music classes. Instead, at the government school we had teachers who were past retirement and who fell asleep in the classroom, teachers who were more eager to keep order in the classroom than to teach. They were more eager to put you in your place and gladly shunned you after school. I do not remember having one conversation with any of my teachers at the government school. What I did learn, I still carry with me. I learned shame there, as they pulled our hair and checked it for lice. I learned silence there, as I stood in line and watched the teacher pull a girl's hair to keep her in line. I learned fighting there, as we channeled our energy the wrong way, for we took our frustrations out on one another. There was no positive regard or positive re-inforcement, only suspicion and mistrust.

Despite it all, I had a favorite teacher in that school run by the Bureau of Indian Affairs. This teacher, a black man or "ha sapa," as the people called him, "skin that is black," was considered a "waśicu," a "black 'white' man." He seemed to belong to that category of "white man," and Kah-kah said that in all his manner-isms, this person, the "black man," seemed closer to the waśicu than anyone else on the reservation. He was the first and only black person I remember seeing in my early life. My world back then was only Lakota and waśicu. It was said that at one time, the black teacher had brought a wife, a son, and a daughter to the reservation. They left, but he stayed. I know how he must have felt as the only black man in our midst; for many years I was the only "Indian" in the classroom in rural Nebraska.

I liked him because he was my first teacher on the reservation, and my first year there I celebrated the whole year. I celebrated because it was the first time in my life that I was not the only "In-dian" in the classroom. All the girls and all the boys were just like me. They had hair, skin, and eyes that were the same color as mine. They spoke English as I did, some better than others. I looked at my friends, cousins, and other children at the school with happy eyes. They were kids who had families like mine, who lived in houses like mine, "miye s'e," meaning "just like me." I finally be-longed somewhere.

This soon gave way to the realization, even as a young child, that a prison is a prison, no matter how pleasant it may seem, and I know that I soon realized that while we lived within the confines of the reservation, we were all under the constant eye and super-vision of a benevolent but neglectful government. I soon realized that the isolation we all felt made us despair silently and that it drove some adults to alcohol and others to insanity. We children, at least, had the school to distract us; for the adults there was noth-ing, day after day. My father didn't stay on the reservation, and in that he was like other fathers, and some mothers. They had nothing there; only the patient ones, the old ones, the children, and those who clung to the old ways could find comfort in the land, the language, and the occasional powwow or dance celebrating some event. For anyone else, the reservation and its schools were a black hole in which your energy is eventually drained. By the time I left the government school in seventh grade, I was a shadow of the happy little girl who had gone skipping out to play at recess in fourth grade. I had become silent and belligerent, but I did not despair.

I had known freedom outside the reservation, and I knew that if I just bided my time, I could someday leave and find something more. I was ready for something to restore me. I wanted to grow stronger, to replenish my spirit, which I knew was on the wane. I could go forward at that critical age, or I could succumb to what others, who were in the same place I was, did. Some tried suicide, others tried alcohol, and still others dropped out of the government schools and followed their parents somewhere, to Denver or Minneapolis, to get away from that demoralizing place called the government school. I was one of those kids who didn't play a sport in school, but I wish I had. I needed to vent my energy in some way. My way was as always in the realm of thought, and perhaps books would have offered me solace. But we had no library; music and art would have consoled me, but they didn't offer those things at that school.

The only music I remember in the government school came from the kindergarten classroom where a senile teacher often sang. Her favorite song was from the *Wizard of Oz*. She would sing, "Somewhere over the rainbow, blue birds fly." When I hear that song, I can still see the tall gray-haired woman in kindergarten who, perhaps because she was somewhat senile, was the happiest person on the teaching staff. She would sing as she wandered from her classroom to the principal's office. When she wasn't singing, she was fond of napping.

The other person who loved music was our fourth grade teacher, the large black man whose baritone voice rang out, "Nobody knows the trouble I've seen. Nobody knows but Jesus." We played tricks on him. We knew that he would not punish us in any way, that he was the only one who seemed to have a sense of humor, so we played harmless tricks on him. One of our favorite tricks was to have someone stand behind him when he sang one of his favorite songs, which was often. He would stop whatever he was doing and lean back in his desk chair, close his eyes, and break into song. We would have someone creep up behind him and have that person pretend to shine the bald spot on the back of his head with the chalkboard eraser, keeping time to the song he was singing. He would always catch on after a few stanzas of his song, when he opened his eyes and saw us all giggling. He would reach behind him to grab whoever was there. His singing seemed to break the monotony of the long days we spent at our desks. He seemed to know that if he sang, we listened and joined in, by being playful in our own way. I liked him because he allowed us to be kids in his classroom.

There were many things that my old school in Nebraska had that I missed at the government school I attended on the reservation. I missed the smell of new books that seemed a natural part of my life in my old school; the clear sound of the triangle when the music teacher played a note to get our attention for music class; the Friday afternoon art class when we could bring bubble gum to class and chew it while we worked unhurried and unsupervised on some art project. Somewhere between my old school and my new one, someone had made the judgment that books, music, and art were no longer important, but I knew they were and I missed them. I remember the year my older brother gave me a pad of drawing paper and charcoal for my birthday. I was already in junior high, but, I felt as if I was back in that sunny classroom in Nebraska, in first grade, when I took a large blank sheet of paper and a new box of crayons and sat down to create something. I don't remember that same freedom in any classroom in the government school.

In contrast, my first year at the Catholic school, I listened to Haydn, Bach, and Mozart. The volunteer the nuns hired at fifty dollars a month plus room and board brought out an ancient record player and played classical music while she had us rest our heads on our desks. I remember "Poppa Haydn" the best. I was in seventh grade at the school, an adolescent ready and able to learn, despite what the government school thought I could or could not learn, what I should or should not be exposed to, what freedom I should or should not be given, even with a simple box of crayons and a blank piece of art paper.

My teacher, a balding woman in her thirties, brought new things to us: she brought books and music—but not art. Her specialties were books, music, and composition. I wrote my first short story for her. I wrote about a ghetto where a young boy died when he broke his promise to his mother to stay away from drugs. The last words he spoke were to his mother, to whom he said, "I'm sorry I broke my promise." The story was called "Broken Promise." I remember it because I wrote it after I had pilfered my older brother's book about a boy growing up in a ghetto and had read it in secret.

It was a time when I was like an empty vessel, ready to hold whatever was poured into me. It was also a time when I realized that I had the power to pour into myself those things that I thought were interesting and new. I "borrowed" my brother's books whenever I could. I read about Hiroshima in secret, suffering nightmares about my skin melting like butter and not being able to die before it happened. It was a time during which I covered my ears when I heard the nightly news because I didn't want to hear the body counts of how many died in Vietnam that day. It was a fearful time, to be in seventh grade, in knee highs and dresses that were one inch below the knee, and feel that the world I read about in my "stolen" books was much more interesting but terrifying than my own.

It was there at that school, in that small valley with the large cottonwood, apple orchards, and statues of the Virgin Mary, that

I found the freedom to enjoy all the things in which I have always felt a certain solace: especially books, but also music and art. I was now able to learn, finally to read and write well; "Owagaȟniġe," meaning "I understood." I also learned how to converse with my teachers in a playful way. The teachers I was exposed to at the Catholic school were not government employees; they were real people. They came to the school to volunteer their talents for the grace of their church, and they were real.

In my second year there, I was finally given a teacher who was an artist. He became my mentor, my substitute for my older brother, who no longer had time for me. My brother had married his high school girlfriend, and they both went away to college. I needed someone to replace him, and this teacher who had come all the way from the East Coast, from Schenectady, New York, with his young child and wife, became the perfect replacement. In secret he called me "wanaȟca," meaning "flower or blossom," and he tended to me like a careful gardener, just like my older brother had done in his own way.

My teacher-friend taught me many things, but one of the most important things I learned was from watching him, how he vented his creative energy. I remember well how he seemed to have a deep well within him from which he drew the sweetest water. He was able to go off alone and come back with something he created, something beautiful and admirable, whether it was a simple water-color, a poem, a story, or a piece of dry wood that he had cleaned and varnished. In whatever way he chose to give expression to his creative tendencies, he always produced something tangible to give or share. He gave me many things, but the most important thing that he gave me was time, the time he spent talking to me.

I liked sitting in his living room and swapping stories with him. He listened well. No matter when I showed up at his door, he would sit down with me and we would talk. The house he and his wife and small child lived in had two bedrooms and a large kitchen and living room combination. They had one couch, an armchair, and a kitchen table and four chairs, which was all that could fit in the small space. The things he seemed to cherish the most in his living space were his books and his music—there were stacks of books and records everywhere. To me, he seemed rich in the things he had, and I have tried to imitate him in what I fill my house with today.

I know now that the most important thing he taught me, neither of us had known then. He taught me in his direct and honest way how to converse in English. He spent time with me, time that up until then no other "wašicu," or "English-speaking person," had. I admired that in him, his acceptance of others who were different. He insisted that we were not so different, the Lakota and the Irish-Catholic. He had been to Ireland, the Ireland that James Joyce had written about. He even made a list of the similarities between what happened to the "Indians" in America and to the Irish in Ireland. He talked about concepts like oppression, things about which I had not heard before. It was not until after he had died, many years later, that I understood what he had told me about his people and mine. I often wish that I could go back to his living room, back to that time, only with the knowledge and understanding that I have now, and have a real conversation with him.

I remember the nuns who ran the school. The women, some of whom had been orphans before coming to the convent, had turned to the church to give them families. They cooked wholesome foods, taught literature, and celebrated the mass among themselves without the Pope looking over their shoulders. I liked their clear minds, practical nature, and calm faith. I respected them, and deep inside I wanted to be one, to have that freedom to be what they were—teachers, cooks, administrators, or whatever it seemed they wanted to be. I liked their mass, a celebration of faith that didn't require you to speak in tongues or dance in the spirit. I liked the quietness of their beautiful church, and the way the priest broke the bread and you had to say, "Lord I am not worthy to receive you, but only say the word and I shall be healed."

I did not always like them. I remember a time before I went to school there, the time my cousin and I went to see them. I remember the face of the nun in the doorway. Her bright, clear, white complexion and red cheeks. Her head covered and her eyes peering through her wire glasses. I remember my cousin knocking on the door and waiting expectantly. I stood behind her, feeling somewhat apprehensive. I was never sure whether I would stand there long enough to be seen or run and hide before they answered the door. My cousin, who was my age, waited very confidently and patiently. Her patience was a source of comfort for me. We were best friends. I was her opposite—flighty and ready to laugh or giggle at the drop of a hat, or run at the sight of a strange dog. She, on the other hand, always maintained a quiet and calm demeanor, her face expressionless. We looked alike, everyone said. I didn't think so. We both had long hair. We were both thin and sometimes we both seemed thoughtful, but our faces were different. Her Lakotaness was real, mine a mixture of French and Indian. My chin was too pointed and my eyes too expressive.

The day we knocked on the nun's door, my cousin was there at the bidding of an older woman, a relative who was indigent. Her husband had asked her to leave their home, and she did, leaving behind a son. She lived here and there, all alone and always looking hungry, perhaps like Iktomi. I feared somewhere in the back of my mind that I might turn out like her. She stood waiting behind a tall cottonwood tree, hiding. The woman had asked my cousin to ask the nuns for some food, to tell them that we were hungry. We were supposed to say not only that we were hungry but to ask specifically for a "cheese sandwich." I hated cheese sandwiches.

When one of the nuns answered the door, she looked at us. "Yes?" she asked expectantly. I stepped back one step, and my cousin began to speak. "May we have a cheese san-witch?" she asked. I turned red and suddenly felt hot and uncomfortable. I didn't want a cheese sandwich. I wanted to know what was inside the convent. They were mysterious to me, the nuns and the priests that we called "sapu" or "they that wear black." I was not Catholic. I had been baptized as an infant by the "ska ų," meaning "they that wear white," the Episcopalians. I knew nothing about the nuns. I was curious, and I wanted to know. I would have my chance a few years later to see exactly what was in that convent, but that day when I stood at the door, it was the first time in my life that I had the opportunity to see a nun up close. I was surprised at how young she seemed, how impatient and human she seemed when she abruptly said, "Just a minute," and went back inside. Within a few minutes she came back out with two cold cheese sandwiches. She handed them to us without hesitating and was ready to close the door. My cousin took them and turned away after saying "thank you." I stood there, as if I had seen a ghost. I waited for something terrible to happen to me, but nothing did. I had just encountered something that I had not expected. She was just as human as any of us, that nun who answered that door. "Next time, why don't you cook for them," she said loudly to the woman who stood hiding behind us somewhere. It occurred to me years later that had I felt confident in my ability to speak English, I would have told the nun about her, the woman who had us beg for cheese sandwiches for her. I would have asked the nun whether she felt it was appropriate for a Christian to tell someone who obviously had no food and was hungry to cook for herself. I wanted to pull the nun out of that door, away from that large white house called a "convent," down the neatly graveled road to the place that the woman lived, to the places we all lived. I wanted to show her what it was like out there where we lived, where for some of us, American cheese and white bread were a luxury beyond words. I stood looking at the door after she closed it and left, and I wondered how I could tell her those things, how I could communicate so that she would know the things I wanted her to know, the things I thought she should know about us. "I could not speak English," back then. "Waśicuia owakihi śni."

I'll Play the Drum for You

In our culture the word "olową" is next to sacred: it means "song." In our culture, music is everything. Just as we send our voices out in daily prayer, we send them out in daily singing. I have heard stories of men and women singing honoring songs, love songs, and even death songs. I have heard them sung, and I have sung them in my dreams. "Blihemiciyị na walową kte yelo," Kah-kah, my grandfather, would say. "To make my heart feel good again, I will sing." So it is, "He hecetu," that when we hear our songs we feel good deep inside where those same songs live within us. When they rise to the surface, we feel whole. Our songs and our dreams are closely tied together. Sometimes songs come to us in dreams that we sing for the rest of our waking days, songs that our relatives identify with us, as ours, and they sing them after we die. Through them we live again.

I remember an aunt and her husband who sat me down one day next to a drum, a "cąceġa," which translated literally means "wooden kettle," or "drum." They said they would teach me to sing a song. They selected six or seven other girls as well, including their youngest daughter, and made us all sit in a circle. Then they gave us drumsticks, "icabu," we call them. The circle, formed by folding chairs, held two places of honor, one for my uncle, who led the group in song, and the other for my aunt, whose voice complemented her husband's. We seven girls filled in the circle,

our young voices eager to fill in the void. In our culture there are
no voids. There is a place for everyone, "Hel iyotaka ye," in the
feminine voice, someone would say. "Sit down there." We leave
no empty places, especially around the drum. If there is an empty
place at the drum, you take up the drumstick and sit down and
join in the singing. "Hel op'a ye," someone would say. "Join in,
take part in it." We are like that—we leave no empty spaces, especially around the drum.

Our all-girl drum group was a creative thought that my aunt
had had, a unique idea. We were a group of young girls who one
day found ourselves picking up the drumsticks my aunt and uncle
had brought with them and began singing. We were new, and un-
usual. We were "woimagaga," meaning "entertaining." People
chuckled or laughed when they saw us. They pointed and smiled,
but they listened when we sang. We could sing only one song, and
that with the help of my uncle and aunt. Left on our own, we
could not play or sing; left on our own we stared blankly at the
drum and fell silent.

It was my uncle who would assume his position at the drum
and miraculously bring out music from the silent drum. He would
take his drumstick, and within seconds music filled the air as we
followed his every move, imitating him with every beat of the
drum. He showed us how to beat the drum without striking its
edge, which would have made a hollow sound and hurt our arms.
He showed us how to follow him if he chose to continue the song
instead of stopping. He assumed his rightful position as leader and
teacher. He never showed any impatience; he just kept trying until
we sounded right. All we did was follow his lead and keep trying.

My aunt, on the other hand, had her own style. She did not
touch the drum. She sat next to my uncle and instead of following
his voice at the pitch he sang, she sang an octave higher. She would
sometimes begin on her own but always at a pace that kept rhythm
with my uncle's voice. "Wicaglata," we call it when a woman sings
like that. They complemented each other. They had been together

a long time, and they had sung together with many other drum groups, most of them far better than ours.

I remember our first public appearance as a drum group. It was at a powwow held in the elementary school gym near our high school. I remember my uncle setting up the drum and handing out the drumsticks to each of us. I remember preparing for the event that night at the high school. One of the girls put mascara on my eyelashes. I usually did not wear make-up, for I shunned anything that smacked of being feminine. I avoided make-up as if it would burn into me. I was afraid I would forever wear dark smudges around my eyes and my brother would laugh at me. I thought that if I wore make-up, it would somehow make me vulnerable to others' opinions. I did not want to be labeled, but somehow that night my friend convinced me that I looked pretty in mascara and I let her lob inches of the black glue onto my eyelashes. It was the night I discovered I had long eyelashes that my friend envied. It was the night I first felt the drum in my hand.

I sat down at the drum after my uncle set it up on the bright clean floor of the school gym. I remember the stares and the smiles. My uncle and aunt had no ego, to bring us out like that and risk their reputations. I admired them for taking that risk. I remember sitting down at the drum and looking around at the group of girls in their mid-teens: fifteen-, sixteen-, and seventeen-year-olds at the drum. We looked exactly like what we were— young, inexperienced teenagers. My uncle put on his wide-brimmed cowboy hat and picked up his favorite drumstick. "Ho" he said, meaning "now." He signaled the first beat, and soon his voice rose strong and experienced. My aunt's voice followed behind his, and then I heard myself singing. The music emanating from the drum and from me was no longer meaningless. It suddenly made sense. It sounded clear and strong. I understood, I felt the rhythm, and I followed my uncle's masculine voice with my own boylike warble. I felt it. It was in me, and it had been in me all along. I had just not allowed it to come out. At first I felt it in

my throat, and I tried to cover my left ear with my left hand the
way my uncle did to better hear myself. But soon I didn't have to,
because soon I could feel it coming out from every part of me. I
could hear it everywhere, and it was my voice.

I had repressed the music all those years that I danced self-
consciously in the dust, in Nebraska, in my heavy buckskin dress.
I had not heard it like I was hearing it at that moment when we
first sang for the public. I could feel the people watching, and I
could feel myself watching. I knew that whatever happened that
night, I would never again hear the drum without watching the
drummers, knowing what they were going through at that moment their voices merged. The drum, that night, became for me
what it had been all along for my uncle and aunt. It awakened in
me a sense of connection. I was no longer the skinny girl with long
hair. I was, at the moment I began playing the drum, connected
to all the others singing at the drum. With it, through it—we were
all connected. Each time we lifted our drumsticks and they landed
on the drum, the reverberation I felt in my hand traveled from me
to the other drummers, from us to the people watching, from
them back to us, and finally from my outer self to my inner self. I
felt the resonance in my hand. It traveled up my elbow to my
shoulder, then to my chest and my stomach and down to my feet.
I felt, for the first time, what the dancers felt when they lifted their
feet lightly to the beat of the drum. As I held my head bent slightly
forward, I felt it—the physical sensation of being connected. I was
being pulled in. I wasn't playing the drum; it was playing me. It
took me by the hand and played me. I felt it deep within; its rhythmic beating was my heart pounding, through it my heart made
itself heard, and with it my voice made itself one with all others.

I have heard the drum many times since then but never like the
first time I heard it. I have heard the drum played at other powwows. I know the difference between the powwow drum and that
which I have heard at our religious ceremonies. I have heard the
drum in the "inipi," or "sweat lodge," at the Sun Dance, at
"yuwipi" or "binding" ceremonies, and at funerals, and even at

peyote ceremonies. I have heard it also on certain nights when I
know that there is a yuwipi ceremony somewhere on the reservation. Even when I am a thousand miles away, I hear it.

Our yuwipi ceremonies are when we come together and lose
track of time in song and prayer. It is a period when we enter the
womb of time and emerge on the other side whole and happy, like
we used to be. I know that in those moments when the people on
the reservation begin praying and singing with the drum in the
yuwipi ceremony, I hear it and feel it. Sometimes I can see them
in that darkened room, their faces and minds merging with mine
into one consciousness through song and prayer. When the ceremony is over, we say "Mitakuye oyas'į," meaning "My relatives, I
pray for; all of them, I pray for."

It was said that in the old days the word "yuwipi," meaning
"bind" or "bound," referred to a round transparent stone found
on an anthill. It is a stone untouched by man, a sacred stone. It
had the power to heal and to foretell the future. It had other pow-
ers, too, and if I lost something that I valued I would consult one
who had a sacred stone. Sometimes, it was said, these stones were
painted the four sacred colors, signifying the four winds: black for
the west, red for the north, yellow for the east, and white for the
south. It was these stones that were used in the yuwipi ceremony.

I remember the yuwipi ceremony Mom-mah had for me when
I came home from the military. It is a yuwipi ceremony I remember well, even before the time they said it was against the law to
practice it, we did it anyway. We drove forty miles from our house,
back through the country roads to an isolated log house in the
middle of a flat prairie near the Nebraska state line. The house
stood there where there were no trees, nothing to break the wind
from howling through the cracks in the windows of the log house.
The house belonged to the family of a "yuwipi wicaśa," "a man
who knew the old yuwipi ceremony." He is called the "iye ska" or
he who speaks, "the translator." He is able to translate what the
spirits say.

The yuwipi began after the men had participated in an "inigaġa," a purification ceremony. The men, including my older brother, came in, and the rest of us joined them in the log house where all of the furniture had been removed. We all sat on the floor. There were several families there. We were all related in one way or another. I remember one older cousin who was afraid and insisted on sitting next to Mom-mah. I sat next to my cousins, who were close to me in age. I sat with them, quietly laughing and talking, waiting for the ceremony to begin.

In the center of the empty room, an altar was prepared by the yuwipi wicaśa. He placed four empty coffee cans filled with dirt in the four quarters of the room, each facing a certain direction. In each can was a flag that signified the four sacred directions: west, north, east, and south. Around each flag were the small ties of tobacco that Mom-mah and others had prepared ahead of time. They were tied in a long string at one-inch intervals and were called "cali opʻaħte." Mom-mah had prepared four hundred of these small bundles of tobacco. She prayed while she patiently and quietly prepared them. I tried to help. My fingers felt large and awkward as I arranged a row of the small squares of cloth. The cloth matched the four sacred colors used in the flags. In the old days, they used small squares of died leather. I filled each square with a pinch of tobacco and tied it with the string. These are offerings to the helpers the yuwipi wicaśa would call upon during the ceremony.

In the altar area, the yuwipi wicaśa places the sacred stones, along with a pipe and other things he needs for the ceremony, on sage, which lines the floor. While he is doing this, we all prepare ourselves for the ceremony. We are given sage, which we place behind our right ear. We also remove all rings, earrings, anything that we are wearing that is made of metal and put them away until after the ceremony. Things made of metal, including eyeglasses, are foreign to the spirits, and so we put them away so that they don't disappear. The spirits might take them. It is at this time that my older cousin, the same woman who had us beg for cheese sandwiches for her from the nuns when we were small, becomes afraid and moves closer to my mother. We all chuckle, but we understand. When the ceremony begins, the lights will be extinguished and the room will be pitch black. We will not be able to see our hands in front of us. This is the way it is in the yuwipi ceremony.

A singer and drummer is present at the ceremony. He usually knows all the songs in which he leads us. We all sing. The songs he sings merge into one another throughout the ceremony. The yuwipi wicaśa fills a sacred pipe with tobacco before the ceremony begins. He speaks to us in Lakota regarding the ceremony. While he does this, we break sprigs of sage into smaller pieces and rub the sage upon ourselves, from the tops of our heads to our feet. The sage will keep the bad spirits away from us during the ceremony. Once the yuwipi wicaśa is done filling the pipe, another man helps him. He binds the yuwipi man in a hand-made star-patterned quilt and lays him face down on the sage in the center of the altar. The light is turned off in the room. The singer begins immediately to drum and sing. His song rushes in with the darkness.

At first, I felt alone in the darkened room. I shifted my body in the darkness, hoping to elbow a nearby person, to touch someone else to remind me that I was not alone. Somewhere in the room was Mom-mah, my older brother, my aunt, my uncle, and my cousins, but I didn't know in which direction. In the darkness, I felt incredibly alone. But when I joined in the singing, I suddenly felt whole. I no longer felt that I was sitting alone in a darkened room on a hard floor. I became aware of myself straining forward to join in, to be a part of the ceremony, to merge with everything and everyone around me.

The yuwipi song that we had all joined in singing awakened something in me, something ancient and familiar. I was not afraid. I listened to the song with my heart, forgetting what my mind was telling me—that time had taken from me, from all of us in that room, all that the old ways required that we remember in order to remain whole. Through the ceremony, I only remembered the strength of the Lakota words in the songs and the sound of the drum. How timeless these things were—the masculine Lakota words in the songs and the sound of the wooden kettle, the drum. The songs we sang called the spirits to us, to the man lying in the center whom they alone can free. We called the spirits, "k'ola," meaning "friend" in a masculine way.

At the point in the ceremony when the spirits entered the room, I remember feeling stronger and more alert. I heard the buffalo spirit come in. "Hutopa," a "four-legged spirit," came stomping through the room, breathing loudly in a sacred way. I remember the spotted eagle entering the room, its wings flapping as if it had landed right on the altar. I have heard them come in and circle the room and thought I had seen the walls of the house collapse and free us, all of us sitting in the room. It exposed us to the cold night sky. I thought I saw, in the wide open sky, millions of stars shining brightly on us. I saw the flickering of the light in the darkness as the yuwipi man was freed from the quilt in which he was bound.

The ceremony in real time is long, and were it any other event, the night would drag on into the morning hours. But in the yuwipi we sing, we even dance, and most of all we pray. When it is over, we emerge renewed as we share the sacred pipe after the last song is sung and the lights are turned on. When the lights come on again, we see that the yuwipi man is free. His helpers have come to assist him in all the ways they have helped since time began for us. During the ceremony they brought healing, they brought news of the future, and of things lost, and they brought answers to questions asked.

It was then, when it was legal to practice these old rituals, that Mom-mah asked the yuwipi wicaśa for a new name for me. It was then that he gave me a new name. While we were dancing in the ceremony, I had felt someone's hands reach for mine in the darkness. A man stood in front of me. He reached for my hands and held them. He moved closer to me and guided my hands to the deep scars on his upper chest. The scars I felt beneath my fingers were the same kind that I had seen when I was a child on the exposed chests of the male Sun Dancers. In the old days, when a man revealed his Sun Dance scars, it was a sign that a person could trust his word. When the ceremony was over, the yuwipi wicasa gave me a new name, Wa suta Wašte Wį, which means Good Warrior Woman. I had been on leave from the military when I came home that autumn. I had been in the Marine Corps. It had been a good and honorable thing to do. Wa suta Wašte Wį is a name I will keep until I die. Although I prefer Badger Woman, my childhood name, when a song is sung for me today, they will insert into the song "Wa suta Wašte Wį," my adult name, and everyone will know that Good Warrior Woman is who I am now. When I hear that name, I will remember the scars of the yuwipi wicasa.

Wild Plum Trees

We eat wild plums in the late summer. They are a small fruit that is both sweet and sour unless it is fully ripe. When I was small, I used to eat plums before they were ripe. I picked them and poured salt into the palm of my hand and dipped them in the salt and ate them, spitting the pit out on the ground. My favorite fruit is the chokecherry, when it is ripe, in August. It is the best treat on a summer afternoon. My mother always warned us, "Tezi niyazą kte kśto," she would say. "You will get a stomachache if you eat too much." I never listened. I picked and ate ripe chokecherries until my teeth were stained black. They grew everywhere near the creek, and it took less time to find them and pick them than it did to hunt for wild plum trees.

My mother had buckets of black chokecherries that she picked in the late summer. She kept them in large brown paper bags until she found the time to prepare them for drying. She used a meat grinder to grind them, pit and all, and made them into small patties, which she dried in the sun. Sometimes she would do it the old way, using a large flat stone as the base and a smaller stone, the size of her fist, to pound the cherries. I volunteered to help when she prepared them in the old way. I liked the noise the stones made when I pounded the cherries and the sound of the pit cracking under the stone. Once dry, chokecherries keep well and are used for special feasts or ceremonies. A puddinglike dessert called "woźapi" is made with cornstarch, water, and sugar using the dried chokecherries. The cherries can be boiled and strained into a juice for ceremonial purposes. The wild plums are also dried, but the pit is squeezed out of the fruit before it is dried, and it is also used in the same way. I don't like the wild plum as much as I like the chokecherry, especially when it is first ground and its juice is sweet and has a nutty flavor from the pit.

My mother remembers all the things her mother did, including the way they went wild-turnip hunting in early June. She remembers how they harvested, peeled, and braided the wild turnips into long strands for the winter. The wild turnip is the size of a large radish but has a dark brown shell that is peeled away to reveal a white inner vegetable. It is sinewy and tastes chalky and strong. It is used in soups, like a potato. In June I have seen the hillsides glow at sunset from the whitish-green leaves of the wild turnip. We find them by the color of their leaves and the small purple flowers on the plant. If you put a spade into the ground right where you find a plant and dig down about seven inches, you will find the dark brown bulb. It has a long root like a slender tail, and when you peel the outer shell, it can be braided in bunches of twenty or more. When braided, it looks pleasing to the eye and can be hung like an ornament in a kitchen or doorway, or perhaps on a tipi wall.

My mother knew how to do all these things, how to harvest wild turnips, ripe chokecherries, and plums, and even how to store them for the winter without refrigeration. She knew these things because she grew up connected to the land and to her mother who told her how these things are done. In the same way, I watched my mother and tried to learn the things she did. She told me that in the old days, if I was to be industrious, hospitable, and true to my husband, that it would have been her task to teach me the proper way. If I were a young woman preparing for womanhood, I would have had to undergo the proper ritual to insure that I would not go the way of the dreaded Anuk Ite Wį, the Wįyą Nupa pi ka, or "the two-faced woman," called Double Woman. The Wįyą Nupa's ways are slovenly and contentious. It is said that her ways lead women astray, and their men are forced to pull their knives out and mark them by cutting off the tips of their noses to signify that they are adulteresses.

It was believed that when we young girls are children before our first menstrual flow, we are no different from our brothers and male cousins and are allowed similar freedom to play and delight in childhood. I remember those times when I ran down the side of a hill, chasing my younger brother and male cousins who ran and hid in the chokecherry bushes. We played cowboys and Indians and captured our enemy, pretending to tie their hands behind their backs. We girls were the "Indians" with our long hair flowing. The boys were the cowboys with their short-cropped hair and jeans. They threw long lassos using rope they stole from my mother's clothesline. They captured imaginary bulls and cattle, which they herded across the creek, splashing in the water and chasing the minnows into deeper water. I remember one game where my younger brother was caught on a ledge. I rushed headlong down the side of the hill to help him, only to find myself trapped on the ledge with him. One of our cousins ran for help, which was about a mile down the hill, past our favorite creek where we played our games and waded in the shallow water. We all played together, male and female, without regard for ability. We ran racing here and there, swimming in the creek, sometimes naked, especially as young children.

Then sometime in my early adolescent years it all changed. I remember the day it happened. I was swimming in the swimming hole we called "Beaver's Dam." It was indeed an old beaver's dam, and the water there was deep enough for us to dive into. I remember the swimming hole well; it was down a bank, about a quarter of a mile from our house. A trail led from our house to the swimming hole and continued on past the swimming hole to another relative's house. The water there was always cool, and the smell of that plant we call "ceyaka," or "wild mint," is strong in the shady spots where it grows along the water. I remember the water spiders skittering across the water and the fish we called "mud suckers" swimming in the dark water. I was terrified of water snakes, but I knew that the more noises we made and the more of us there were, the more likely that the snakes would stay away. I liked trekking though the woods with my younger brother and cousins in tow, on our way to swim away a summer afternoon.

Then one summer I bled into the creek. I ran home and shook as I told my mother what had happened. "Wįyą nikuže kśto," she said. "You have the 'Woman's sickness.'" She quietly helped me as I undressed out of my wet cut-off jeans and T-shirt. She bought a contraption called a "belt" and gave it to me along with a box of clean-smelling white pads. The pad she gave me had what looked like long handles, which she told me I was to loop through the belt and wear. I didn't like the awkward and uncomfortable looking thing, but I wore it anyway. She told me that I must dispose of it properly because if I didn't, I could bring illness upon myself or others. She told me other things that I needed to know as well. She said I must never step over a person sitting on the ground but should walk around. She said I could no longer walk over things, such as an article of clothing on the floor or someone's shoes, but that I must step around them. She said it was especially disrespectful for a young woman to step over people or things. She told me that I could no longer leave my hair on the hairbrush and carelessly throw the hair away. She said the hair on the brush must be disposed of properly: it should be burned in a fire but never allowed to touch the ground, which would be a sign of disrespect for myself. She told me never to leave my clothing on the floor for others to step on. That too would be disrespectful of myself. She told me all these things which had to do with how to conduct myself in a proper manner now that I was menstruating.

She didn't tell me about sex or the new ability to bear children, the way they would have in the old days in the old rituals. She perhaps looked at me, a thin knobby-kneed young girl in cut-off jeans and hardly a chest to show, and felt that I was physically still far from those worries. When I look back, I realize how quietly I accepted what she told me, I did not ask why it happened and what it meant. I was aware that she had had her menses and that other women had theirs, too. I knew that it was my time, and I accepted it as such.

In the old days, before it was illegal to practice our rituals, I would have undergone the appropriate ceremony that would have answered for me all the mysteries of my first menstrual flow. The proper rituals or ceremonies were important to us. Every phase in our lives had its own ritual or honoring ceremony. "Kici glu onihą pi ye," Mom-mah would say. "Honor each other." In my culture children are precious. Each child is considered a gift from Wak'ą T'ąka, an answer to a prayer. Our people prayed for children, and when a child was born, its well-being meant everything. We made vows and offered sacrifices to insure our child's safety. Sometimes we publicly stated, "Wak'ąyeża ki he tewaȟila," so that the people would know and understand: "That child is precious to me." In the old days certain ceremonies were done to show that love. Through them children learned that they were loved and honored. They learned how to honor themselves and others.

We believed that our thoughts had power, and it was important always to be aware of our thoughts in all matters. If someone was in mourning, it was said that they were "wak'a," or "sacred," and that they had to remain aware of their own sacredness by having the right thoughts. If someone was on a vision quest, he had to focus all of his thoughts on prayer and on what it was that he was seeking. For us, life was determined by one's thoughts. So everything was done to instruct the young and impressionable at an early age. Being a young girl, I would have been especially vulnerable to those teachings. It was in the whole tribe's interest to impress upon the young female mind the right thoughts, the right teachings, for it was believed that where the woman goes, so goes the tribe. It is the woman who determines the fate of the tribe.

In those days it was believed that spirits took possession of my body as a young girl and made it bleed. These spirits returned each month after the first month, causing me to bleed until I satisfied them by becoming pregnant. Then they would leave me for awhile. It was also said in those days that embedded in the bloody products of my menstrual flow was a power so great that I should be banned from the presence of others on whom I could use this power for good or evil. It was for that reason they isolated us from the tribe during our menstrual flow.

We were sent to a place called "isna ti," a place where we lived alone, apart from our families. "Isna ti" means "alone she lived." There, it was said, "wążįni kįyela ų kte śni," or "not one person should come near." We stayed there until the cycle ended, and then we were free to resume our lives as before. While I dwelled in the isnati, I had to dispose of my menstrual waste properly, hopefully by putting it into small bundles which I then carried and placed upon a wild plum tree. It was said that the spirit of the living tree would guard the bundles and that the plum tree was a desirable place to leae them because it was fruitful. Its spirit would bless me with many children. If I did not dispose of the bundles properly, the coyote would find them and give them to Iktomi, who would then use them to turn my thoughts and influence me to do disgraceful things. It was also said that if I had a husband, I should not sleep with him while menstruating, or else, it was said, I would sleep with the coyotes and my children would be a disgrace to me. When the flow ended, I would leave the isna ti. I would purify myself by bathing in an "inikaġa pi," or "sweat bath ceremony." After being purified in this way, I could then rejoin my family.

In those days the first menstrual flow was cause for a ceremony, one in which it was affirmed that we Lakota are indeed "Pte Oyate" or "Female Buffalo Cow People." In that ceremony I would go to the isna ti with my first menstrual flow, returning to the tribe after an inikaġa pi, and then I would undergo a T'atąka olową pi, or a Buffalo Ceremony. There I would be instructed on my new role as a woman.

Certain things must be done for the T'atąka olową pi. First and foremost, a medicine man is invited. "Opaħa k'u pi," that is, "Tobacco is given to him," as a way of asking him to officiate at the ceremony. My mother and father would send invitation wands made of wood to guests whom they wanted to attend the day-long ceremony. To those whom they did not want to come, they would send a dry bone. They would then prepare for the ceremony by making or obtaining a new tipi, and a new dress and breechcloth for me. They would bring to the new tipi, which is put up with the door facing the east, or the direction from which all knowledge and wisdom comes, a new wooden bowl, chokecherries, sage, sweet grass, "kŋiknik," or "dried chokecherry wood shavings," dried cottonwood or box elder wood, an eagle plume, a pipe, a drum, and food and gifts for the guests. They would pray for a good day, a day when the west wind would keep Wakṟyą, the dreaded "Thunder Being" away and the skies would be blue and clear. When everything was ready, a fire was made at sunrise the next day and the ceremony began.

It is said that all the items brought for the ceremony are placed in a spot in the tipi, "catku ta," which is always "the place of honor." Inside the tipi, everything is done in a circle. Catku ta is a place on the west side of the tent, directly across from the entry-way, which faces east. There a mound of earth is placed, which signifies "Mak'a," "the Earth." On this mound is placed a buffalo skull, which overlooks everything we do, for we are the Pte Oyate, or "Female Buffalo People."

I would play my part in the ceremony had I lived then, as other young girls millennia before me had done, by placing my menstrual bundles in a living plum tree, cleansing myself physically and spiritually in the inipi, and entering the prepared tipi wearing the new dress over my old one, along with the breechcloth under my clothing. I would have worn my hair loose down my back to signify that I was in mourning for the death of my childhood.

When the ceremony begins everyone is seated in the tipi in a circle, with the men on the north side and the women on the south side. The medicine man enters and begins the process through which I would learn, by observation, all that I needed to know to be a buffalo woman. Upon entering the tipi, the medicine man would look over each person, making sure that everyone there was of good character. He would take his place on the west side of the tipi, catku ta, and would begin the ceremony by purifying the air, first with sage and then with sweet grass. The smell of sage burning would remind us all to clear our individual and collective thoughts. We believe that spirit is mind; therefore, when the mind is purified of all dark thoughts, the spirit of the ceremony is purified as well. We believe that the scent of sage burning is offensive to "bad" spirits and keeps them away from the ceremony. It permeates the air wherever it is burned.

When I smell the sweet pungent scent of sage, I know I am in the company of my ancestors who believe in all the things I have started to believe in. They believed as my mother does, that bad spirits are negative thoughts and that sage reminds me to clear them from my mind. "Śicaya wiyukca pi śni ye," Mom-mah would say. "Do not think bad or negative thoughts." She said I should watch my thoughts carefully, to make sure they are free from judgment and other impurities. When she was feeling downhearted, Mom-mah would say, "Śicaya wiblukca he u," or "I feel this way because my thoughts are impure." She said they made her feel physically weak.

In the T'ataka olowa pi, after the air is purified, a ceremonial pipe is smoked by all who are present. The medicine man takes a puff of the pipe and blows it into the buffalo skull that sits upon the mound of earth in the tipi. He then paints the forehead of the buffalo skull red, to signify the buffalo people are one. He inserts into the mound of earth two wands with tobacco ties, small bundles of tobacco tied in dyed red leather. He does this to please the Creator. He then sings a song, "Buffalo bull in the west, lowing. Buffalo bull in the west, lowing. Lowing he speaks." While he sings, at the beginning of the ceremony, I sit cross-legged like a boy. At the end of the ceremony, Mom-mah comes and takes me by the hand and I stand; when I sit again, I sit the way she sits, like a woman, demurely, with both legs to one side.

The medicine man prays for me, sprinkling sage, cedar, and

sweet grass upon the fire. I can hear the crackling of the cedar as it burns and the smell of both permeating the tipi and my mind. The medicine man prays that I will be a good buffalo woman and have many children. He prays that I will heed the spirit of the buffalo and remain true. He prays that I will be truthful, loyal, and firm of character. He prays and tells me that he saw good things in my future, like a spider, a turtle, a meadowlark, a brave man, many children, and a tipi with welcoming smoke pouring out the top.

He prays and tells me that he saw bad things among the good, bad things like a coyote and worn-out moccasins. These things he explained to me, saying that I should be industrious like the spider, wise and thick-skinned like the turtle, happy and kind of voice and spirit like the meadowlark. If I lived like the spider, the turtle, and the meadowlark, I would find a good brave man and have many children. My husband would provide me with buffalo hides to make a tipi where all would be welcomed with true Lakota hospitality. These were the good things he saw in my future. If I failed to live like the spider, the turtle, and the meadowlark, and chose instead the opposite of the qualities they represented, I would be lazy, poor, and miserable, and live among the coyotes. I would wear worn moccasins, and no man would either marry me or provide for me the buffalo hides for my own tipi. No man would paint his dreams upon the walls of my tipi.

The medicine man would then turn his attention to teaching me proper sexual conduct. He would instruct me never to be intimate with a man unless I intended to be his wife. He would imitate a buffalo bull in heat and approach me, as if I were a young buffalo cow. My mother would step in front of him with sage in her hand, using it to ward him off. He would approach me several times in this manner, and each time my mother would step in to protect me with sage in her hands, which she then placed upon me. I watch, fascinated by what he is doing, feeling embarrassed and somewhat ashamed of my new role as one who can arouse him, the buffalo bull, this way. They continue with the ceremony, trusting that I am ready to know these things, even if I do not fully understand them, even if I do not yet know that my fascination and embarrassment are elicited to protect me.

When the ceremony is almost over, the medicine man hands me the two wands he had placed between the horns of the buffalo skull, and I take them. These are my "medicine," and they will help me. The wands have the small red tobacco pouches tied to the ends. It is these that I carry with me. Even now, when a ceremony begins my mother brings hers with her to make sure that her thoughts will remain pure, like a buffalo woman.

The medicine man offers everyone a drink made with boiled chokecherries strained into a juice. We all drink together, and then I stand and take the new dress off that I had worn over my old, and I give it away, to signify that I have given it to the buffalo spirit. My mother then parts my loose hair down the center and braids it into two neat braids, the way a Lakota woman wears her hair. The medicine man paints my forehead red. He also paints the part down the center of my head, from my forehead to the nape of my neck. He tells me that red signifies all that is good and that I may, from that day forward, paint my face the way he has to signify that I am a buffalo woman. He then takes the eagle plume and ties it to the upper back portion of my hair. Although I would not yet fully understand what being "a buffalo woman" meant, had I lived in that time when these ceremonies were done for us this way. I know that I would understand somewhere deep inside where everything that I am is the color red. After he tied the eagle plume to my hair, he would finish the ceremony with a song: "A man from the north gave me a cane. I told this girl so. She will live to be old. Her tribe will live." It is a song that has been sung for my mother, her mother, and her grandmother. It is a song that binds me to them.

My Grandfather's Sak ye

Mom-mah said that my paternal grandfather had a "sak ye," pronounced "sah-ge," meaning "cane." She said it was a beautiful sak ye, beaded entirely from top to bottom. She said that it was painstakingly done in a geometric design. She admired it the way she admired my father's father. She had great respect for him. "Wicaśa waśte heca," she said. "He was a good man." She admired the things he had, that cane and a house that he bought and lived in, in that small town in Nebraska. He did not rent a house the way everyone else did; he bought one. I remember that house. I saw it long after he died. It sat abandoned in our old neighborhood. "Ti ska," my mother called it, "the white house."

Once I asked my father how he met my mother. I did not have the courage to ask until later in my life, after they had been together again following one of his long absences. He said he met her at the fair in Nebraska where I had danced in my buckskin dress at the rodeo. He said he had gone there for the rodeo, carrying his own saddle. It had been a habit of his to follow the rodeos with only his saddle, winning prize money and traveling from place to place. In the same way, he registered and rode in the bronc riding event at the fair in Nebraska. He said that while he was there his sisters arranged for him to meet a young woman seven years his junior, whom they said might be a good wife. They liked this woman, and they wanted their only brother to meet her. They wanted him to settle down, and they thought Mom-mah would be the best person to convince him to do so. He said he asked his sisters, "Which one is she?" and they pointed her out. She was standing near the rodeo grounds at the county fair in Nebraska. He remembered thirty years later how her hair was red in the August sun, and how that somehow pleased him. In my father's seventy-fourth year, when he lay sick and dying of lung cancer, the wife his sisters helped him choose remained near him, comforting him with her quiet presence. When he died, she missed him. Once, when she was very ill, she said she woke up and saw him lying next to her the way he did all the years they were together.

I think about my paternal grandfather's cane, his sak ye. How patient that person must have been to bead that cane from top to bottom. I asked Mom-mah what happened to it. She said that when he died, his things were given away, as was customary, and she didn't know who took it. I wonder, even now, who has it today and where it is. When I think about his cane, I think about all those things that we Lakota have lost through time, the things that I have lost in my childhood, in my lifetime. I have heard that it is only in time that we can lose those things that are finite. Those that are infinite, we never really lose.

Mom-mah said she wishes that she had a picture of my paternal grandfather. She said there were many pictures of him, but that they disappeared after his death. She remembers the pictures of him sitting on his beloved horses. How grand he looked on those horses. "Yupiya yą ke," she would say. "He sat 'well' on his horse." I don't have any "thing" by which to remember my paternal grandfather. I did not inherit his "things," neither his horses nor the land that he and my grandmother owned. Those he left for my father. When my father died, I was sent an inventory of his "trust/restricted title holdings" that showed he had owned 256 acres of land in Rosebud, among the Brulé. His estate was awarded less than $2,600 for the land, or about $10 an acre. My grandfather's landholdings were much larger than that, but over the years my father sold his inheritance, sometimes for a lot less than $10 an acre. I once tried to buy ten acres on the reservation, offering to pay $100 an acre, trying to buy back what my father sold. Perhaps it was too finite, this land that my grandfather and father had owned, because through time, they lost it.

We Lakota seem to lose "things" that way—our lands, our way, our language, and even our religion. The lands that we lost which we remember the most are the He Sapa, the Black Hills. If you look on a map, you will see them, in the lower part of the state on the western end near the Wyoming border. Those are the hills that I remember as I traveled to them from the plains. I did not grow up near them. I had to travel north through the Badlands to get to them, and even then, it was only to visit the city at the edge of the hills. Once a month or so, I would travel a few hours north toward the hills, feeling excited as I saw their outline to the north-west. I was not excited because the hills meant anything to me but because I enjoyed the small city in the foothills. In all those years, I did not know that those hills belonged to my people.

I remember the first time I spent four days in the Black Hills. The Catholic high school I attended took all the juniors at the school to the Black Hills for a retreat. They loaded us all into a school bus, and we traveled north along the eastern edge of the hills. It was the farthest point I had ever traveled into those hills. I remember the bus creaking up the steep incline as we climbed a dirt road. When we arrived, I was surprised at the beauty all around me.

It was the first time I heard the wind in the pine trees there in the He Sapa, the wind whose essence my people had tried to cap-ture in song and prayer. For me, it was like putting my ear to a seashell for the first time and hearing the wind in it. When I heard it in the He Sapa, I thought I heard the hills breathing, the way the old ones used to say "ąpao t'a niyą" to refer to the morning mist. They say the day catches its first breath as seen in the mist rising in the early morning sun. In the same way, I thought I felt the breath of the Creator in that wind.

I sat in my room during the retreat on my first overnight trip

to the Black Hills and contemplated, the way I was supposed to.
What I thought about was not God and my relationship to him,
as the Catholics wanted us to do. I thought about the land and my
relationship to it. I thought about the Creator, the Lakota One,
the one that Mom-mah called Tʻųkašila. I thought about Him and
how he created the Black Hills, these hills outside the window of
my room. I thought about the Creator's breath in the wind, how
he seemed to want me to know how intimately I was connected to
these hills, to everything outside my window.

I saw the sun light bouncing off of the needles of the pine trees.
How it glimmered like nothing I had ever seen. I watched all of it,
and I thought about why I had never seen or heard these things
before this. I know now why I had never noticed or thought about
the Black Hills the way I did as I sat in my room on that retreat,
near a place called "Bethlehem Caves." I know now that the government had succeeded. They had succeeded in wiping from my
generation's memory any connection to those hills, the Paha Sapa,
the He Sapa, the dark hills. They wanted us to forget that they had
ever belonged to us. The government took them when gold was
discovered there in 1874. Even now one of the largest gold mines
in North America sits at the northern end of the hills. The land
there is stripped bare and flattened out in segments, like stairways
that look like pictures I have seen of Aztec monuments built to
appease their many gods. It was for the gold that they took our
hills, even after they had signed a treaty saying that they would be
ours as long as the grass was green.

Growing up, I did not like the Black Hills. I saw them as a tourist trap—a place where tourists came and bought trinkets made in
Japan, dyed feathers and tomahawks, and where they had a chance
to pose with an Indian in a war bonnet. I associated the Black Hills
with Mount Rushmore and all the other tourist attractions there,
and I felt no real connection to them. I had forgotten what my
ancestors knew, how sweet the smell of the pine is in those hills;
how clean and clear the skies are in the Black Hills; how gentle the
sun is in the shade of the pine trees; and how the flowers compete

with the butterflies in the summertime. It was said that the spirits of the flowers make the rainbow after a summer rain. How intimately my ancestors knew all of the plants and animals that lived in those hills. They knew how sacred the bear was that lived in these hills, because only the bear could walk on its hind legs like a man, a "hu nupa," or a "two-legged." It was the bear who taught us what medicines we could use to heal our sick.

They wanted us to forget that our ancestors had roamed and hunted in these hills, especially in the winter. In the winter our people found shelter, wood, and game there. In our legends it was said that the hills were a figure of a reclining woman, and our people went there like children, to feed upon her breasts. In the early spring and summer, they had places in the He Sapa where they came on pilgrimages to fast, pray, and ask for guidance from the Creator. Like the Christians returning to the Holy Land to follow in the footsteps of their ancestors, we Lakota came to the Black Hills to appease our God and give thanks for everything— all the mysteries of life. To us it was the center of our universe. Today, when I return there, I feel the loss. I know now what those hills meant for my people.

When I see them today, I feel the need to reclaim a place in them, just as I feel the need to know where my grandfather's sak ye is, the beaded one that Mom-mah had been so proud of. The He Sapa, the Black Hills, to this day are lands that my people lament the loss of, just like my paternal grandfather's cane, his sak ye that Mom-mah talks about. How beautiful it was. I don't know what else my grandfather had owned, whether he had a favorite hat or scarf. He was fond of wearing red scarves around his neck, like a cowboy. Perhaps it was the French in him. There are many things about my paternal grandfather, my Kah-kah, that I wish I knew. One thing I do know is that he had a cane that was beaded from top to bottom in a bold geometric design. In the same way, I know that the Black Hills once belonged to my ancestors. When I go there, I look at them, feeling a need to go back there someday to live. It is there, to the Black Hills, that I want to bring my chil-

dren and my grandchildren. It is there, in the He Sapa, that I want
to tell them about their people, about my paternal Kah-kah, my
maternal Kah-kah, Mom-mah, Keg-le, my brother, and all those
who have traveled the wanaġi cȧku, the spirit road. It is there, in
the dark hills, that I want to go to spend my days when I grow
old. But, then, I remember how these things go, how the finite is
lost in time and the infinite, the spirit of our ancestors and all that
they loved, is never lost but remains there.

We retain even now our connection to the spirits that live there.
The energy in a thunderstorm; the lightning when it touches the
edge of the forest where the hills end and the treeless plains begin;
the sound of the thunder cracking over the hills; the sight of the
sun rising over the plains; the sunbeams in the pine forest; the
sound of the meadowlark; the snow that falls quietly there. These
are things that will always be ours, because they belong to no one
but the Creator.

Sitting on Red Cloud's Grave

We would climb the hill, past the old church with the buffalo painted on the high ceilings, and walk up a dirt road to the cemetery. The road was the one they used for funerals. I had never been to a Catholic funeral until I went to that high school. One of the students died, and our whole class went to the funeral. He died on a weekend, and they buried him during the week. He was a junior. To me, it seemed he had a lot of promise. He was my cousin. My father and his father came from the same ancestor, Chief Lone Elk, a Brulé. My father's and his father's grandmothers were sisters. His father had been an artist who depicted life among the Lakota in the early part of the century. He tried to show what it was like for the reservation people. I remembered how my father and I went to visit his family. They lived in the same small town in which I lived in Nebraska. When he died, it was hard to believe that I had just seen him in our homeroom the Friday before. They said he had been shot by a bootlegger. It is illegal to sell alcohol on the reservation, but it was well known that there were certain houses in town where one could buy liquor. At his funeral, the priest burned incense, and we all stood unbelieving while they nailed his coffin inside another box, what we called a "rough" box made of unfinished pine. Over that they slowly shoveled dirt. They buried him on the other side of the highway where the newer cemetery was. It was the first and last time I went to that side.

I knew the old side, the side where Red Cloud is buried. The old side was where we went on slow afternoons, after school let out and all the day-students went home. Those of us who boarded at the school had free time between three o'clock and five o'clock. We would check in with the matron, the older woman who was in charge. Then we would buy a candy bar at the snack stand the nuns had in the recreation room, and if the weather permitted, we walked up to the graveyard. Our lives at the school were regimented to breakfast, school, lunch, school, free time, five o'clock mass, dinner, study hall, free time, bedtime, and lights out in the dorm at ten o'clock. The only block of free time we had was that time when we could walk up to the cemetery, sit down, and talk. It was the only private place, the only spot where we could be irreverent and no one would hear us. We found solace there as we grew older, and our lives changed from the shallow and frivolous years as freshmen to the somewhat more mature introspective years as juniors and seniors. The time I remember the best was my junior year.

It was my best year at that school. I went there, following in my brother's footsteps. He honored Mom-mah and Kah-kah by finishing second in his graduating class. As always, I had a more difficult time. It was not that the studies were hard; they were not, as I was able to prove to myself in my junior year when I won awards in my classes, signifying that the teachers gave me the highest honor. I had not expected it and was working at the library the night they had the awards banquet. My friends came running to tell me that I should have gone to the awards ceremony because my name had been called out for the different awards. I was surprised and pleased. The small gold pins were important to me. My junior year was the year I finally accepted who I was. All of my life, I had been less sure of myself than my brother was.

It was a time when I felt suspended between the safe and sure footing of childhood and the ever-shifting quagmire of adolescence. I felt uncomfortable feeling like that, unable to choose the side I knew best—childhood. When I had first gone to the high school, it felt like I was giving up the things I loved the most about childhood: the games I played, like "Red Rover, Red Rover," in the alfalfa field with my cousins; the comic books we kept in brown paper boxes under our beds and read over and over; the cold days when we played jacks and cards on the kitchen table in the lamplight, when the days grew shorter in the winter. My favorite cousins grew up in the log cabin near where Kah-kah had lived most of his life. They had no electricity. I remember dancing to Roy Orbison on a portable radio. It was those cousins I missed the most when I left home for the first time to board at the Catholic school. It was they who in their Lakota ways embraced me when I first came to the reservation. We played, pretended, dreamed, laughed, and joked in Lakota. They will always remind me of those carefree times I enjoyed as a child, before I had to go away to boarding school.

I had to leave home like the kids that they stole and put into boarding schools when Kah-kah was growing up, only I went voluntarily. It was one of two high schools on the reservation, and by the time I was ready for high school, I knew that I would go to that school named after Red Cloud. They said that he was buried there in the graveyard of the "Sapa ų pi" or "they that wore black," which is what Kah-kah called the Catholics. Kah-kah was a "Ska ų pi," or "they that wore white," which is what someone from the Episcopal church is called.

Red Cloud, who was buried in the Sapa ų pi cemetery, had first invited the Catholics to the reservation. He chose the land where our reservation was established; he and a Brulé chief named Spotted Tail selected the sites where our respective reservations now stand. Red Cloud invited the Sapa ų pi to educate the generations that would call this place home, this small area of land far from the Ḣe Sapa. He knew that these generations, including my own, would never know the kind of freedom that he and Crazy Horse and Sitting Bull had known. Red Cloud knew that our spirits would be subdued by this place, by the reservation. He wanted freedom for us, the kind that only they knew. So, he invited the

Sapa ų to give us freedom of a different kind, that of the mind, for we Lakota believed that mind and spirit were one and the same.

He knew that in the time after the Sapa ų were summoned and had come to build their school and church, that we Lakota, being a spiritual people, would naturally embrace them. He knew also that in this new world forged by the government, our physical selves would be limited to the boundaries set by the reservation, and we would fare better if we were educated. He knew that our spirits would never accept this limited life, the way he tried not to, even when everything fell apart and our people were ordered to abandon forever their way of life. In the years I attended the school named after him, I never knew how much foresight he had had, how much he understood what life would be like for my generation.

I remember those autumn days after school, how the light seemed dimmer and the air colder as we trekked up past the headstones to our favorite spot at the graveyard. I don't remember stopping to read the other gravestones. We didn't have time for that. We usually walked directly to the gravestone at the far eastern end, where the entire grave was covered by a cement block that stood about three feet high. It was our favorite spot because we could all sit on it side by side, looking off toward town, watching the cars come and go.

It was a favorite pastime for the town kids to cruise the road between the school and town. We watched the cars coming and going until we saw the five o'clock bus returning from town, which meant that if we wanted, it was time to go down to mass. The group of us sometimes went to the five o'clock mass with the volunteers who lived at the school. They were our teachers, some of them young Jesuits and priests. We liked our teachers, and they seemed to like us. So we sought them out. We joined their mass, and they invited us into their circle where they held hands as they sang along with a guitar. If we didn't go to the five o'clock mass, we would get ready to go to dinner. It wasn't our favorite thing to do because the food was lacking in quality. The cook at the school believed that fresh baked bread was not good for you, so he kept the bread in metal garbage cans until it was quite stale. Next to the stale bread, he always served up some main dish that no one ate. His assistant was a Puerto Rican man from New York City. Between the two of them, they cooked very unappetizing meals. I stopped eating meat altogether and became a vegetarian.

I worked part-time at the library, and I would find time during the week to log in hours, for which I was paid. I liked my life there. If I wanted to borrow money, I would go to the Jesuit who everyone knew kept a set of books for that purpose. He would pencil in my name and the amount I borrowed, usually less than five dollars, and then when I came back to pay him, he would take a ruler and cross out my name. He kept his books meticulously, and I liked the way he puffed on his pipe when I came to borrow money for the weekend and the way he never declined my request. I liked the predictability of the place: the dorm, the library, the dining hall, the school bus ride home on the weekends, and the way I never felt I lacked for anything there, except a sense of the real world.

When I was a freshman at the school, the math teacher, a woman from New Jersey, announced that she wanted to invite four students from our school to try something new, to go home with her to teach the Lakota language and culture at the high school where she had taught the year before. She said the four students selected would go that summer, in early June, returning in time for the annual Sun Dance in August. I remember sitting in the gym when she made the announcement at the student assembly, the one we called the "little boys' gym," a term left over from the old days when the younger kids boarded at the school, too.

Mom-mah had boarded there as a young girl. She hated it. She said she admired the older girls who grew proficient at throwing large buns at the nuns when they turned their backs. They were given freshly baked buns for a snack, and many of the older girls kept theirs until they hardened. Then they used them as missiles, which they launched and fired at nuns they didn't like. She said by the time the nuns turned around in their heavy habits, the girl hurling the bun was standing silent and still. She said the hardest thing about her experience there was kneeling for so long at mass. She said sometimes she would use one of the hats they were given to wear at mass as a cushion for her aching knees. By the time I came to the high school, the nuns no longer wore habits, except for a stubborn few, and the younger students, those below the ninth grade, no longer boarded there. Everything had changed. The Lakota language was being taught by Lakota teachers, and the requirement to go to daily mass was no longer in place. We still attended mass on all the Catholic feast days, but the church was no longer an integral part of the school. It was no longer forced upon us the way it had been for Mom-mah.

The math teacher made the announcement and recruited students to fill out applications for the four slots. I filled out an application and handed it in, not really thinking about what it meant, other than the fact that it was a fully paid summer job. A summer job was important in our family. It was one of the only ways I was able to afford school clothes and a decent jacket to wear in the fall. At the next student assembly the math teacher announced the names of the four students selected, along with an alternate if one of the four declined. I was chosen among the four. When my name was announced, I felt uncomfortable being singled out in my group of friends. I did not want to bring attention to myself.

My friends were very familiar to me. We had been together since elementary school. All of our parents spoke Lakota, and our last names were not English or French like the half-bloods at the school, but Lakota. Our Lakota last names, combined with the fact that we came from isolated communities, meant that we were somehow different from the half-bloods. The difference was subtle, which made life even more complex for us. We were a group of full-blood Lakota girls whose self-image was determined by many other factors, not excluding this one. It was one more difficulty that my older brother had not had to deal with. He played football, liked politics, and could easily pass for an "iye ska," what Mom-mah called the "half-breeds." It means "translator," a name carried over from the time many of their ancestors translated Lakota for the government and English for our forefathers. I, on the other hand, looked like what I considered myself to be, a full-blood Lakota adolescent, floundering in a non-Lakota world. It was a time when I still thought in Lakota.

When school ended in my freshman year, and before I had a chance to breathe, I began my new job with the math teacher. I wasn't sure what going away from home for a summer job would mean, but I knew that I would be homesick. I had never been away for very long, at least not that far away. The night before I left, Mom-mah came to see me. My brother, six years my senior, drove her to the house at the school where we were staying, just before we were to begin our trip east. Mom-mah brought me a small cassette recorder. My brother, who was home from college, gave me a tape of Buffy St. Marie songs. I knew they had both scraped together all the money they had to buy me those things. I hugged Mom-mah and said good-bye, promising that I would write often. "Iyokśice śni ye. Iyokpiya omani ye," Mom-mah had said. "Do not be sad. Travel with a glad heart." I did not want my older brother to see the tears in my eyes. I was glad it was dusk when they came to say good-bye. I watched the taillights of their car grow dimmer as they pulled away on their way home. I knew that I could very easily have refused the summer job in New Jersey and stayed at home, but I went even though I was homesick before I left.

That summer, I felt like Red Cloud on a tour of Washington DC. I saw everything with intensely curious eyes. We drove east in a small Ford Mustang. Five of us, including the math teacher, squeezed into that small car loaded with our belongings. We made our way to New Jersey via Milwaukee, Chicago, Detroit, Charleston, Washington DC, and finally New York City. I do not remember being fond of any one city except for Washington DC, as I ran through the museums and monuments, feeling happy to be on the go. By that time, the four of us, two of us freshman girls, a freshman boy, and a sophomore girl, felt at home together. We all had known one another at the school by sight but not as well as one would think in such a small school.

When summer ended, we drove home. We had accrued experiences that no one on the reservation would believe that four kids from our high school could have had. We had even spent a week on Cape Cod and been to the shore along the Atlantic coast in a small yacht. My summer had been full of everything from my first banana split to my first taste of champagne and caviar at an art gallery near Cape Cod and even a small cup of wine shared with the cast of a play on Broadway in New York City. When I returned that autumn to the high school, I felt embarrassed when the math teacher showed slides of our experiences that summer. I had forgotten that I was coming home to high school at the end of the summer, and how I had acted as if I were a tourist on vacation. I was embarrassed by my own expectations after my summer there. I looked around me, at the kids in that small classroom, and realized how foolish I had been that summer, that my life was probably never going to be that way again.

I realize now that the year after I went east was a turning point for me. It was then that I became restless. I wanted something more, and I was never really sure what it was until I went away to college. I didn't realize that the morning I loaded my gear in that car and headed for the East Coast, that I would never really unpack my suitcase on the reservation again. I would, from that day forward, always look for the next opportunity to leave the reservation and see what lay beyond its borders.

I left the high school for a semester after that. I went to live with my older brother in a city near the Black Hills. I lived with him and attended the high school there. I did not like the school but kept going because I did not want to be labeled as a "dropout." I worked part-time at a local motel as a maid, cleaning rooms and changing beds. I knew I had to stay in school. If I didn't stay, I could expect only jobs like the maid's job I had that winter. I wanted to return to the reservation, back to my old school, but I had left because of fighting there. An older girl, an "iye ska," had taken a great dislike to me, and rather than fight, I left. I did not like the violence that erupted when the kids drank alcohol. I did not readily accept violence. I had inherited Mommah's gentle heart, and although I had been involved in fights, I felt greatly dishonored by any violent act. I could not comprehend what it meant. I remember when an older girl gave me my first bloody nose. She jumped me while I was viewing exhibits at a science fair. I felt dazed. How unreal it felt to feel the thud of skin against skin. I could not understand what it meant, perhaps because I did not grow up that way. It seemed foreign to me.

While I lived, worked, and went to school in the city, my older brother and others were restless as well. A new movement had come into our midst. It was a new political movement that was gaining momentum. My only contact with it was through my brother. I attended a few of the political rallies sponsored by the new movement, but I, like Mom-mah, was cautious and stayed back, not knowing what it would bring for the people in the end. When I look back now, I realize that what it meant for the people in my community was a loss of innocence. I remember the way it was before they came and the way it was after.

In my small community, before the movement came, we were insulated from the world. The boys, including my youngest brother, rode Shetland ponies up and down an old wagon trail that ran next to the highway. It was called the Big Foot Trail. It was named after the chief whose people died at Wounded Knee. The boys raced their ponies along that trail. They could be seen in groups of seven or eight, riding everywhere together. We girls walked up the road on warm summer evenings to the white bluffs across from the community center. I still remember the smell of fresh hay on those evenings. Our families all knew one another. We all lived in houses set a mile or so apart. There were distinct "tiošpaye" or "extended families," and elders who presided over them, both male and female. The local policeman was a very large man with a big belly hanging over his belt. He had a family in our community. Although no one had a telephone, he always seemed to know when someone digressed and had had too much alcohol to drink. We lived like that, isolated but serene in our innocence.

The changes brought by the movement were more apparent during and after the occupation of Wounded Knee in 1973, when followers of the movement barricaded themselves in a Catholic church there in a stand-off with the federal government. I can still see the federal marshals in their blue suits, toting guns and coffee as they milled about in our community. I was a high school student, and I watched it all in silence. When the occupation was finally over, someone came to Mom-mah and asked her if she would smuggle one of the leaders out in her car trunk. Mom-mah said "No," not because she was against them, but because it was wrong. I admired her for that, and like her, expected life to be like that, everything black and white, right or wrong, innocent or guilty.

Now that I look back on what happened to my community, I realize that because we were so close to Wounded Knee, we were all indicted. We were all guilty of aiding and abetting. Whom? I was not sure because from where Mom-mah and others in our community stood, both sides in the stand-off were at fault. Rightfully, we felt like the pawns that we were in that conflict. Once we perceived that, we lost our innocence.

The time after the occupation, chaos came and settled in our midst. Guns and drugs became available. Life grew more complex. Mom-mah came close to being wounded when she stepped into the line of fire in a drive-by shooting as she walked out of our post office. She was fortunate that the bullet only grazed her forehead. A few years earlier, I was not so lucky. I stepped right into the line of fire when someone who had access to a gun began randomly shooting. The bullet went through the right side of my chest. I survived, although at the time I thought, as only an adolescent would, that I had done something wrong even though I had been only guilty of being in the wrong place at the wrong time. These things happened after the occupation of Wounded Knee in 1973.

It was a time when these occurrences seemed common, "wo kope ya," Mom-mah would say, "frightfully so." A few days after graduation ceremonies were held at my high school, I was shot. I didn't attend the ceremonies, vowing that I would attend my college graduation—a seemingly impossible dream for someone coming from where I did.

It was a Sunday morning, the morning I woke up and thought I was going to die. Someone was randomly shooting a gun, and I awoke to find everyone in the house hiding on the floor. They were trying to dodge bullets flying through the house. I didn't believe or couldn't believe what was happening, and while I stood in a half-awake stupor, I felt something tear into my right chest. At first I thought it was happening to someone else; then I realized it was happening to me. When I began to bleed, I did not want to lie down. I thought if I did, I would never stand up again.

What I learned from that experience was that I was no longer safe there, in that place I had taken for granted as my childhood haven. At the time I was shot, I was an adolescent coming into young adulthood, and that fact put me into a category I considered more dangerous in that place. I knew I had to leave.

Long before this event occurred and I was still in high school, I had contradictory feelings about the movement, particularly during and after the occupation of Wounded Knee in 1973. On the one hand I identified with those who supported it, and on the other hand I did not like the violence. I did not know then that I would be directly affected by the violence that I so disdained.

When everything was over and the leaders of the movement were on trial or in jail, I felt guilty. After all, they had come to fight for us, for the full-bloods, the traditional people. When I wrote the following poem, I felt solace in the fact that they taught me something after all. I did what I knew best: I watched and waited,

gleaning as much knowledge as I could from what I saw, the way
Lakota children are supposed to learn. I wrote this poem for them:

Up on top of the prairie hill where sky meets earth,
High among the pine trees where the four winds blow,
A generation, lost in its search for identity, is asking,
"Who are we, we need to know. We have to know."
Descendants of people with an unwritten history,
So the answer was hard to find.
Only the old ones who preserved the history in their memories
    seemed to know.
Confused they turn to the ones who remember,
"Grandfather, show us the way, the road that will lead us all
    home."
Perhaps the answer lies hidden in the past.

Grandfather teaches them the ancient ways so they may not be
    forgotten.
He points out the road, but he refuses to lead.
He spoke these words to them:
"Do not walk backward for you will surely fall.
Learn from what is past, but look to tomorrow's dawn and
    follow the sun.
Walk frontward and learn of the white man's ways, of his
    writings, his books, and his language.
But most important, learn to walk side by side with him, as a
    friend.
Perhaps his books will tell you what you wish to know."

The generation listens to his words for he does not speak
    foolishly, as all old ones are wise.
But when he finished, some turned their backs and closed
    their eyes and refused to see or hear.
Others bravely walked ahead, straight and tall.
The four winds warned, "Do not separate. You are brothers
    and you are strong, together, as one."

It was too late. The words were not heard.
Those who walked ahead were over the next ridge.
They did not bother to look back, only ahead.
Those who walked blindly and mutely backward had fallen,
    obscure figures in the past.
Grandfather stood alone. He sang a mourning song, high on
    the hill.

I wrote the poem as a senior at the Catholic high school, and
the Catholic Church paid me twenty-five dollars for that poem
and used it in their mailings. Their mailings were what my older
brother called "begging letters" and were part of what he had
disliked about the school. Back then I did not mind. Even if my
understanding was limited, I felt that I understood. My brother
had Kah-kah and Mom-mah to turn to in his arrogance. When he
first discovered that the Catholic school was sending out the letters and had labeled them "begging letters," it was because he had
felt outraged by them. He did not like the words "poor" and "Indian" in the same context. He felt that we were neither of those
things. He knew who he was. I didn't. By the time I finished high
school, Kah-kah had been dead seven years and Mom-mah and I
were no longer living under the same roof. I was on my own, and
I was not so sure what the future would bring.

I was grateful to the Catholic school for providing a safe place
for me to learn and grow. I understood that without it I would
not have known that I preferred John Steinbeck to any other
writer. I would not have known that I could write poetry. I would
not have known that Red Cloud was buried there, and that he,
too, understood these things: how hard it was to be Lakota in a
world where Lakota is not the language of choice. He understood
that although we Lakota children were educated by the wašicu, we
were first and foremost born of Lakota parents like Mom-mah and
my father and that as a result we thought as they did, and still do.

Red Cloud tried to pass on what he had learned in his extraor-
dinary life. At the end of his life, he realized that the true meaning

of the Lakota people rested solely on their relationship to their Creator—"T'ṵkaśila" or "Grandfather." He knew that our meaning did not lie anywhere else and that there was nothing else but this. Red Cloud saw this relationship with the Creator as one of perfect union and unbroken continuity.

He contemplated, in his last days, whether what the Sapa ṵ pi said, was true. How they said that we lived wickedly before they brought their God. Yet, as he watched them, he saw that the relationship they said they had with their God was often contradictory to what he saw. Their religion, to him, seemed partial, self-centered, fragmented, and full of fear. He saw his own relationship with T'ṵkaśila as self-encompassing and self-extending. The relationship he saw among the new religions, including the Sapa ṵ pi's, was self-destructive and self-limiting to the Lakota. He said that when we Lakota relied only on our relationship with T'ṵkaśila and lived according to the old beliefs, which dictated that we demonstrate in our daily lives compassion, truthfulness, fortitude, bravery, and true generosity, that we would live happily and die satisfied. He looked at what the waśicu brought to us, after they put us on the reservation, and he saw how inadequate it was for the Lakota, how insufficient. He tried to convince us that we Lakota had within us our own beliefs, our own relationship with our God, T'ṵku śkạ śka, our Creator. He wanted us to remain true to these things that had been sufficient for us since the beginning of time. The way Mom-mah, Kah-kah, and my brother, six years my senior, wanted me to be true to my Lakota self.

Red Cloud looked forward to seeing his ancestors in the spirit world. He knew that because the Sapa ṵ pi said we had lived evil lives before they came and brought salvation, our ancestors might not be in the waśicu's heaven. He felt solace in the fact that in the Lakota world view—the law of cause and effect—that as long as he remained true to T'ṵkaśila, he would see his ancestors, there where Mom-mah said they lived "cạte waśteya," "with glad hearts."

I remember how the night comes there where there are no city lights, like a thick blanket falling over me. I remember how I sat

on Red Cloud's grave until the shadows grew long. Like any adolescent, I felt invincible in my irreverence. Even Red Cloud's grave
did not seem real to me. I was firmly rooted in the here and now.
I did not know what my future would bring for me. I did not think
about those things. I did not even think about whose grave it was
that I was sitting upon. I wonder, now, as I sat there on his grave,
if I was like a young sapling grafted onto an ancient tree, whether
I absorbed some nourishment from him, my ancestor whose spirit
remains firmly planted there. When I look back now, I realize that
Red Cloud was right, that Tʻųkašila, the Lakota God whom Mom-
mah and Kah-kah believed in, still lives in everything that is Lakota. He knows all things and knows that we are still true to Him.
"Ho he," as Kah-kah used to say, and as Mom-mah says now:
"That pleases me. It is good."

CPSIA information can be obtained at www.ICGtesting.com
Printed in the USA
BVOW11s2319270414

351748BV00005B/8/P